# HOW TO STAY HUMAN IN A FUCKED-UP WORLD

# HOW TO STAY HUMAN IN A FUCKED-UP WORLD

## Mindfulness Practices for Real Life

**TIM DESMOND**

HarperOne
*An Imprint of* HarperCollins*Publishers*

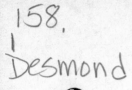

HarperOne

Gatha on page 190 reprinted from *Present Moment, Wonderful Moment*
(1990, 2006) by Thich Nhat Hanh with permission of Parallax Press,
Berkeley, California, www.parallax.org.

FIRST EDITION

*Designed by Yvonne Chan*

Library of Congress Cataloging-in-Publication Data

Names: Desmond, Tim, author.
Title: How to stay human in a f*cked-up world : mindfulness practices for
real life / Tim Desmond.
Other titles: How to stay human in a fucked-up world
Description: San Francisco : HarperOne, 2019.
Identifiers: LCCN 2018039828 (print) | LCCN 2018053324 (ebook) | ISBN
9780062857590 (e-book) | ISBN 9780062857583 (hardback)
Subjects: LCSH: Self-actualization (Psychology) | Meditation—Buddhism.
| Happiness. | BISAC: SELF-HELP / Personal Growth / Happiness. |
BODY, MIND & SPIRIT / Meditation. | RELIGION / Buddhism / General
(see also PHILOSOPHY / Buddhist).
Classification: LCC BF637.S4 (ebook) | LCC BF637.S4 D4787 2019 (print) |
DDC 158.1—dc23
LC record available at https://lccn.loc.gov/2018039828

ISBN 978-0-06-285758-3
ISBN 978-0-06-295433-6 (ANZ)

19 20 21 22 23 LSC 10 9 8 7 6 5 4 3 2 1

*This book is dedicated to every person who cares so deeply about the world that it's killing them.*

# CONTENTS

*INTRODUCTION  1*

CHAPTER 1
**SOMETHING DEEPER THAN DESPAIR**                5

CHAPTER 2
**FINDING BEAUTY IN LIFE**                15

CHAPTER 3
**THE ART OF UNHAPPINESS**                25

CHAPTER 4
**KNOW YOURSELF**                49

CHAPTER 5
**HOW TO STAY HUMAN
WHEN OTHER PEOPLE SUCK**                63

CHAPTER 6
**WHY DO BAD THINGS HAPPEN?**                85

CHAPTER 7
**THE ART OF NOT EXISTING**                101

CHAPTER 8
**HEALING OLD PAIN**                                    115

CHAPTER 9
**YOU'RE NOT CRAZY**                                    131

CHAPTER 10
**BECOMING FEARLESS**                                   147

CHAPTER 11
**COMMUNITY AS REFUGE,
COMMUNITY AS WEAPON**                                   165

CHAPTER 12
**YOUR TEN THOUSAND HOURS**                             177

*AFTERWORD  197*
*ACKNOWLEDGMENTS  198*
*ABOUT THE AUTHOR  199*

# INTRODUCTION

I was sitting in jail in San Francisco with some friends. We were in a holding cell downtown nursing a few minor injuries, but no one was seriously hurt. We'd been arrested together at plenty of protests before, and we knew it'd be a couple of hours before we'd get released. At the time, I was in graduate school for psychology and feeling quite proud that I hadn't "outgrown" my rebellious phase (and as of this writing, I still haven't).

We were killing time by talking about whether we thought the world was getting better or worse. My friend Erik said he believed the world was getting better. He said that if you think about the world in 1850, with slavery, colonialism, the Native American genocide, and the subjugation of women, then the present has to be better. That made sense to me.

However, another friend, Stephen, said he thought the world was getting worse. He pointed out how more wealth and power are being concentrated in the hands of fewer and fewer people, and asked how could things be getting better if there's a good chance the planet won't be habitable in a hundred years. Also a good point.

As they went back and forth, I mostly listened. I'd been around this same debate many times, and it always fascinated me. Both of these diametrically opposed views appealed to me, and I wondered whether both could be true. Could the world be getting better *and* worse at the same time?

I also wondered how my attitude might change if I finally picked a side. If I believed the world was getting worse, would I feel that all our efforts to create positive change were doomed to fail? On the other hand, if I believed it was getting better, would I feel apathetic, like all our work wasn't really necessary?

Just a month earlier, I'd been on retreat, studying meditation with Zen master Thich Nhat Hanh. During one of his lectures, he'd talked about the Buddhist idea of *skillful means*—that sometimes what's most important about a belief system is how it affects you. What kind of worldview would make me a better person? Which would help me stay committed to working for change?

After a lot of thought, I decided there would be a rationale for giving up and one for persisting, in any of these perspectives. Maybe human beings are evolving toward some kind of more enlightened consciousness, and maybe ever since we stopped being hunter-gatherers, we've been destroying every-thing we touch. Maybe both or neither. Ultimately, it wouldn't change what I want to do with my life.

There is a tremendous amount of suffering in our world, and I can't think of a better way to spend my life than by try-ing to leave things better than I found them. That motivation has been a driving force in my life, and it's led me around the world studying meditation in Buddhist monasteries, organiz-ing social movements, founding nonprofits, and most recently leading a mental health startup at Google. My hope in writing this book is to share with you what I've learned, so that it might be of some help to you in our beautiful and fucked-up world.

# CHAPTER 1

# SOMETHING DEEPER THAN DESPAIR

I would not have you descend into your own dream.
I would have you be a conscious citizen
of this terrible and beautiful world.

—TA-NEHISI COATES

On November 14, 2016, just six days after Donald Trump won the election, my wife, Annie, woke up in the middle of the night in excruciating pain. A trip to the ER revealed that the cancer she'd been fighting for more than a year had spread into her abdomen and a tumor was blocking her left kidney. Several long hours later, she emerged from surgery with a plastic tube implanted in her side that drained urine into a bag. I was told that she'd likely have this tube for the rest of her life. When our three-year-old son visited, I had to teach him not to touch his mom's tube.

That was a moment I could hear despair calling me—almost audibly. It said, "Your life is shit. Everything is completely fucked. Your best option is to go cower in the corner."

In that intense moment, I thought of a story I'd heard the Vietnamese Buddhist monk and peace activist Thich Nhat Hanh tell countless times over the twenty years I've studied with him. It's a story about a banana tree and it goes like this:

One day, Thich Nhat Hanh was meditating in the jungle in Vietnam and he saw a young banana tree with just three leaves. The first leaf was fully grown, broad and flat and dark green. The second leaf was still partially curled beneath the first, and the third leaf was very light green and tender, just beginning to unfurl.

This was during the middle of the Vietnam War, and he was leading a huge organization of young people who'd help rebuild villages that'd been destroyed by bombs and napalm. He'd spent nearly every day with villagers whose lives had been ravaged by war, and he'd witnessed the deaths of several of his closest friends. The central question in his life at that moment was how to reconcile the intensity of his calling to help suffering people with his mindfulness practice. He knew that he needed his mindfulness practice to keep from being overwhelmed with despair, but how could he justify cultivating peace and joy in himself while so many other people were dying?

He was holding this question in mind and looking at the young banana tree when he had a deep insight. It occurred to him that the eldest banana leaf was fully enjoying her life as a leaf. She was absorbing the sun and rain, radiating beauty and peacefulness. However, she hadn't abandoned the other leaves to pursue her own happiness. In fact, as she nourished herself, basking in the sunshine, she was also nourishing the younger leaves, the banana tree, and the entire jungle. He decided that

8

human beings are just like this. As we nourish ourselves with peacefulness and joy, we're also supporting the well-being of every other person in our lives.

In that hospital room, as I looked at my wife and son, I couldn't avoid seeing how much they needed me. They didn't need me to do anything in particular. They needed me to stay with them and help them to see that they weren't alone—that life was still worth living. If I could somehow find a way not to lose touch with what's beautiful and joyful in life—if I could tap into something in me deeper than despair—then I'd have something to offer the people I love most.

## DEEPER THAN DESPAIR

Looking around today, it's hard to escape the conclusion that our world is exquisitely fucked. Of course, there's a lot of beauty in the world at the same time, but the sheer magnitude of violence, greed, hatred, and straight-up stupidity can be overwhelming if we let ourselves pay attention and care.

The terrifying part for me is what happens to good-hearted people when we get overwhelmed by all of it. We're committed to paying attention and caring, and we refuse to escape into whatever privilege we can find. However, the intensity of suffering we experience poisons us, and we lose touch with our humanity. We either end up in despair on one side, or we fall into toxic righteousness on the other.

*Toxic righteousness* is a term created by writer and activist Starhawk to describe the anger-fueled self-certainty that pervades our political discourse. Toxic righteousness is what happens when we're mere inches from despair but somehow summon enough strength to lash out instead of collapsing. In that state, we're incapable of listening, and often don't even see why we should, since our opponents are less than human. If anyone tries to say that our vitriol and indignation aren't helping, we get violently defensive because we believe the only alternative is giving up entirely.

The challenge of staying human in a fucked-up world comes down to how we respond to the immensity of suffering that confronts us from every direction. Whether I'm suffering from things in my own life, things in the lives of people I love, or the pain I feel when I pay attention to the conditions in our world (and it's usually all of those), I have to find a way to take care of the compassion in me so that I don't end up overwhelmed. If I can't, I'll find myself in despair, possessed by toxic righteousness, or (worst of all) I'll find whatever little bubble of privilege I can escape into and stop caring.

Once I understand that the suffering in the world can turn me into someone I don't want to be, I become extremely motivated to find a way to stay human. I don't want to stop caring, and I don't want to drown in anger and bitterness. I want to stay present and be a force for good. I want to become Thich Nhat Hanh's banana leaf with enough joy and peace that I'm able to benefit myself and others. I refuse to let everything that's fucked up in the world strip me of my humanity.

## FROM HERE TO THERE

How do I become that kind of person? How do I strengthen that capacity in me? What am I supposed to do if it's not easy for me? What if I really struggle with anger, despair, and shutting down? Is it possible to change?

I can almost guarantee that when I was first exposed to mindfulness and compassion training as a nineteen-year-old college student, I was a much more fucked-up person than you are. I grew up poor in Boston with an alcoholic single mother. I was constantly bullied, homeless as a teenager, and I never knew my father. By the time I got to college, I was angry and lonely, and had few social skills.

When a political science professor of mine assigned *Peace Is Every Step* by Thich Nhat Hanh, it changed everything. I immediately recognized that mindfulness and compassion were exactly what were missing from my life. Then—as nineteen-year-olds sometimes do when they find something that makes sense to them—I immersed myself in these practices, often spending several months on retreat with Thich Nhat Hanh each year and following him wherever he went.

Through all that practice and study, I've learned to experience more joy and freedom than I would have thought possible. I've gone from being someone with an intense amount of suffering and self-destructiveness to someone with real intimacy and harmony in my life. If I can change, anybody can.

## NOTHING IS FREE (UNTIL IT IS)

On the other hand, change isn't easy, and it doesn't happen on its own. It requires that we find ideas and practices that make sense to us on a deep level. We have to engage with those ideas and allow them to change how we see the world. Then we have to put them into practice and see what effects they produce in our lives. Finally, when we find a teaching or training that feels truly helpful, we must commit ourselves to deliberate practice. The more time and effort we invest, the greater the change we can expect to see.

But then something magical happens. The practices and ideas that used to require so much effort begin to feel like second nature. It's as if you've put so much energy into learning to speak French, and then all of a sudden, you realize you've developed a little fluency. You can now have a conversation in French without much effort at all. In this case, we start to experience a compassionate thought arising on its own in a moment that would have triggered anger in the past. It's the fruit of our dedication. It's the effort that leads to effortlessness.

## WORDS GET SICK

It's possible to pay attention and care about the suffering in the world without letting it poison us. There is a quality of mind we can develop that allows us to stay present with suffering without losing touch with the joy of being alive. We can accept that pain is an inevitable part of life without letting that make us callous or uncaring. Instead, we can respond with radical acceptance and a willingness to do whatever we can to alleviate suffering.

The word that my teacher Thich Nhat Hanh uses to describe this way of relating to life is *mindfulness*. However, I don't really like that word. Too many people use it to mean something entirely different from what Thich Nhat Hanh means. They say mindfulness is about taking deep breaths, sitting on a cushion on the floor, or watching your thoughts and feelings with disinterest—like you're watching a boring TV show.

When Thich Nhat Hanh uses the word *mindfulness*, he's describing a way of relating to the world (and specifically to suffering) that contains compassion, joy, equanimity, and wisdom. It is precisely the quality that allows us to stay human in fucked-up situations—to stay open, caring, and able to relate.

It's possible for words to get sick and lose their meaning. When that happens, we can either abandon the word or we can try to rehabilitate it. I'm not entirely ready to give up on the word *mindfulness* (at least not today), but when I use it, please remember that I mean it in this deeper sense.

Regardless of what you want to call it, the ability to stay human in the face of intense suffering is something that's in short supply in our world. It's also something that we desperately need. So the next question is how to develop this capacity in ourselves. How can we learn to do this better?

I've spent my life studying this question, and I've come to believe it can be developed through training ourselves in a set of specific skills. This book is designed to help you develop the skills that will help you stay human—help you pay attention, care deeply, and feel connected—even in really fucked-up situations. First, you'll learn about each skill. Then you'll try it out until you find a way of using it that feels beneficial. Finally, you'll practice it until it feels natural.

# CHAPTER 2

# FINDING BEAUTY IN LIFE

As stupid and vicious as men are,
this is a lovely day.

—KURT VONNEGUT

When life is fucked up, it's so easy to believe that nothing good exists—or even if it did, it wouldn't matter. However, if you only pay attention to what's bad in your life, you will inevitably end up exhausted and overwhelmed, because experiences of joy are the fuel that we need in order to be present with suffering.

Too many people focus exclusively on everything that's wrong in their lives and in the world, and the result is they end up being too burned out to do anything about it. There's a subtle art to learning how to be present with suffering in a way that won't overwhelm you. Most of this book will focus on facing suffering directly, but the first skill to develop is how to find beauty in life. If you can't do that, it will seem like suffering is all there is in the world, and that will crush your spirit. This isn't a practice of "looking on the bright side" or some other way of denying real pain and injustice. Instead, it's an essential skill for staying human.

In every moment of life, there are infinite reasons to suffer and infinite reasons to be happy. Our experience largely depends on where we're focusing our attention. For example, imagine taking a couple of minutes to list everything that you *could* be upset about right now. You'd never run out of ideas. Now imagine taking the same amount of time and making a list of everything that you *could* be happy about, like the sky at sunset, the sound of rain, or the eyes of a newborn baby gazing at you. That list could be pretty long too.

So many of us believe that it's impossible to be happy until all of our reasons to suffer are gone. Yet, we also know that's never going to happen. There will always be reasons to suffer— small ones, like goals we haven't accomplished or people who don't understand us, and big ones, like war, poverty, oppression, and climate change.

These reasons to suffer exist, but they aren't all that exists. For us to have any experience of joy, we need to be able to pay attention to what is beautiful in life in this moment. That doesn't mean we're denying the problems in our lives and in the world. Instead, it means that we recognize how tragic it would be to go through life ignoring all of the beauty and wonder around us. If we put off our happiness until all our reasons to suffer are gone, we'll never have a chance to be happy. If we don't feed ourselves with moments of happiness, we'll have no energy to make the world better.

We can develop the skill of noticing what's beautiful in life by training ourselves in the ability to choose where to focus our attention, rather than letting our minds run wild with worries and judgments. It takes commitment, but if you're doing it right, it should also feel pretty good. We are remembering to appreciate the shapes of clouds, the feel of a cool breeze on our skin, and the presence of a loved one beside us.

## ENJOYING YOUR NONTOOTHACHE

As we practice recognizing what's beautiful in life, we also begin to notice everything that *isn't wrong*. For example, when we have a toothache, it's clear that not having a toothache would make us happier. However, as soon as our toothache goes away, we forget how lucky we are. Take a moment to see if you can actually *enjoy* your nontoothache right now. If your tooth feels okay, try saying to yourself, "If my tooth hurt, this is exactly what I'd be wishing for. I'd believe that I would be so happy if only my tooth felt okay." Experiment with this way of thinking and see how it affects you.

It doesn't make you naive or simpleminded to think this way. It's actually a much more rational way of thinking than focusing exclusively on the problems in life to the point that they make us stressed out and irritable. In every moment, there are infinite ways that life could be a little better and infinite ways it could be worse. Most of us have a strong habit of focusing on everything we don't like about our lives, or everything we want to change. Since this habit can cause a lot of harm, it makes sense to practice bringing more balance into our way of thinking and to make a conscious choice not to ignore all of the conditions for happiness that are present right now.

## PRACTICE

- Put this book down and spend a minute or so noticing all of the conditions for happiness that are present in your life *right now*.
- You can write down your list, or just think about it.
- If your mind gets distracted or resists this practice, try saying to yourself, "My mind believes there are other thoughts that are important, and that is true. However, I give myself permission to think about what's beautiful in my life for just this one minute. Everything else can wait."
- Notice how you feel.
- If it feels good, you can do this several times a day. The more you practice, the sooner you'll notice changes in your life.

## BEAUTY IN THE HARD MOMENTS

As I mentioned earlier my wife, Annie, is being treated for stage 4 colon cancer. She was diagnosed in 2015, just after our son's second birthday. Since that time, we've been through multiple surgeries, chemotherapy, recurrences, and dozens of late-night trips to the emergency room.

One of the most difficult parts of this whole experience for me is waiting for results from scans. I don't mind waiting in the lobby, but once we're called into the doctor's office, we're often sitting there for twenty minutes or more before he arrives, and it's torture. I know that the doctor could walk in at any second with news that might change everything. I brace myself at every sound of footsteps in the hallway.

Annie and I always hold hands during this time. I pay close attention to my mind, doing my best not to get carried away by the stories running through my head. I want to stay present so I can be there for her.

A few weeks ago, we were in our doctor's office waiting for scan results, and I was aware of a powerful thought arising in my mind. It was saying, simply, "No." No, I don't want this to be happening. No, I refuse to accept it. Every part of me was rejecting the reality in which I found myself, as though I might be able to change it through pure force of will. I wanted to be present for Annie, but I was lost in my own suffering.

Thanks to my training, I came back to my mindfulness practice. I closed my eyes and focused all of my attention on the storm of emotion raging in me. I gave myself permission to feel what I was feeling and be open to it.

After a few minutes, it occurred to me to ask myself why I hated this experience so much. The response was immediate—"because I love my wife and I don't want her to die." Obvious, right? Yet, with my mind and body slightly more grounded, it was a revelation. I looked at her and felt her warm hand in mine. I could see that I was in such pain because I didn't want to lose her, because she's so precious to me. Yet right in that moment, there she is, alive and here with me. What am I doing grieving? I was so lost in pain that I couldn't celebrate this real moment of being together. From this new perspective, it seemed like such a waste of time.

When I teach about mindfulness, there's an example I often use to show how the best intentions can go horribly wrong if we're not aware. I ask people to imagine a man who gets cut off in traffic and then sticks his head out the window shouting obscenities and maybe even throws a plastic water bottle at the other car. If we could pause in that moment and ask the man why he's doing that, he might say, "Because that jerk cut me off!" Going a little deeper, we could ask why that upset him so much and he'd answer, "Because it was really unsafe and disrespectful." Oh, we'd say, you want to be safe and respected? He'd say, "Of course." So he was looking for safety and respect by screaming out of his car window and throwing things.

In that moment with my wife, I felt as misguided as the man in this story. There we were, alive and together. The intensity of my emotions was entirely based on how dear she is to me. The only thing that made any sense was to celebrate that moment of being together. I began crying tears of joy. In that present moment, we were alive and the only thing to do was to feel grateful.

When the doctor finally arrived, we got good news. That scan showed no progression in her disease. However, we've had enough good scans and bad ones to know this doesn't mean we're in the clear. In a few months, we'll be back in that same room with no way to predict what the doctor will say. Yet that moment belongs to the future. Right here and right now, we are alive, and I refuse to waste a minute of this precious time. This experience is teaching us to celebrate every moment of life we have.

CHAPTER 3

# THE ART OF UNHAPPINESS

The cure for pain is in the pain.

—RUMI

On October 13, 2011, Mayor Michael Bloomberg of New York City told Occupy Wall Street protesters that they would be evicted the next day to clean Zuccotti Park with power washers. Most of the protesters believed that it was a pretense to clear the park and end the demonstrations. In fact, on *Saturday Night Live* it was joked that anyone who's spent much time in New York City doesn't see a lot of evidence of public parks being power washed.

That night, hundreds of protesters rented industrial cleaning equipment and scrubbed the park while other organizers discussed how to prevent a forcible eviction. A call went out, and in the morning more people than ever crowded into Zuccotti Park.

I was asked to cofacilitate the General Assembly on the morning of October 14 with Nicole Carty, another core organizer of the demonstrations. That morning, the thirty-three-thousand-square-foot park was an ocean of humanity, people of every age and background crammed shoulder to shoulder, all risking their own safety by defying the mayor's eviction notice. The atmosphere was incredibly tense as police in riot gear surrounded the park, penning us in.

Nicole and I were tasked with doing the impossible: facilitating a consensus meeting with thousands of people who were all in imminent physical danger. Our primary role was to communicate information about what was happening, things such as "This is the phone number of the National Lawyers Guild to call if you're arrested." On top of that, we attempted to facilitate a discussion about how the crowd should respond if the police began to advance.

I remember standing on a stone wall, looking into that crowd, and seeing on people's faces the fear and anger that threatened to overwhelm their hope and turn our gathering into chaos. I thought again of Thich Nhat Hanh's banana tree, and I wanted to project as much calm and solidity as I possibly could—to let the mindfulness in me somehow pass into that crowd. That might sound like a good idea, but in reality, I was just as freaked out as anyone else.

I recognized that the fear I was feeling was rooted in thoughts about all of the ways the situation could go horribly wrong. Although my fear might have been perfectly rational, it was also profoundly unhelpful.

I stopped to take a breath, and focused my attention on the sensations of tension and agitation in my body. I gave myself complete permission to feel those physical sensations without trying to change them, and I allowed them to be as strong as they wanted to be. For three or four breaths, they became incredibly intense, but I have enough experience with this practice that it didn't worry me. I spoke to the fear in my body and said, "You can be as strong as you want. You can stay or go. You are welcome. I am here for you."

I felt the tension and agitation in me begin to relax. I continued to breathe and focus on all of the sensations in my body with open acceptance. I said to myself, "Even when you're afraid, you are loved. You don't have to make the fear go away. I'm here for you." And after just a few more breaths, I felt calm and solid.

I saw myself in front of that crowd with the police issuing warnings over their bullhorns, and recognized that there was nowhere else on earth I'd rather be. It was undeniable that bad things could start happening at any second, but they weren't happening now, and me being freaked out was not going to help anything.

Next, I tried saying to myself, "This moment is a wonderful moment." I said it mechanically, and then attempted to find a way to believe it. With my body feeling calm, it wasn't hard. *Of course* it's a wonderful moment. Look at these amazing people who are risking their comfort and safety because they want to create a better world. I fell in love with every person in that crowd, and I believe they could feel it.

About twenty minutes into our General Assembly, we got word that Mayor Bloomberg and Brookfield Properties (which manages the park) had rescinded the eviction notice. The police quickly dispersed as the protesters celebrated. The joy we felt was overwhelming.

As you likely know, this was a temporary victory. Just under a month later, police cleared the park in the middle of the night with no warning at all. However, things don't need to be permanent to be precious. In a long enough timeline, every victory is temporary, so we must learn how to appreciate these moments.

## THE PART OF LIFE THAT'S TERRIBLE

*Not everything that is faced can be changed,*
*but nothing can be changed until it is faced.*

—JAMES BALDWIN

If we want to address any problem effectively, then we must—at least—be able to face that problem without getting overwhelmed. But how do you do that? When we're looking at the suffering in our lives or in the world, it's easy to feel angry, judgmental, or helpless. However, it's also possible to develop and grow our ability to face painful realities with compassion, equanimity, and humanity. You already have everything you need inside you to do this. All it takes is training.

One of the most important skills for staying human is *coming home*. It means learning how to come back to what's real in the present moment, instead of being lost in our worries and fantasies. Some of what's real in the present moment is beautiful, and the previous chapter focused on training ourselves not to forget that part of life. However, some of what's real in the present moment is fucking terrible. In this chapter, we'll learn how to face that part of life without getting poisoned by it.

## *DUKKHA* HAPPENS

After the Buddha achieved enlightenment, he hung out by himself for a few weeks. Then he went to find his friends in the forest and explain to them what he'd just figured out. The very first teaching he offered was the Four Noble Truths, and many people believe it was also the last teaching he gave before he died. There are lots of translations of the Four Noble Truths, but my favorite is by Thich Nhat Hanh. These are his translations (with a literal translation in parentheses):

**Everyone suffers sometimes** (Noble Truth of suffering).
**Suffering has causes** (Noble Truth of causation).
**Well-being is possible** (Noble Truth of cessation).
**Well-being also has causes** (Noble Truth of the path).

*Dukkha* is the Pali word that usually gets translated as "suffering," and most people believe it comes from a term describing a bad wagon wheel. If your wagon wheel fit perfectly on its axle, the term was *sukha*. If it was a bad fit, the term was *dukkha*. So the Buddha didn't use a word that means "intense pain" to describe our universal experience of suffering. He used a word equivalent to "a bumpy ride."

Why would *dukkha* be the first part of the Buddha's first teaching? Why would "everybody suffers" be such a point of emphasis? I believe one reason is because we're generally pretty clueless about whatever we're feeling at any given moment. This is especially true when we're dealing with the shitty parts of life.

For example, I follow a lot of political activists on Twitter. When I see a post about an innocent person getting brutalized by police, the first thing that pops into my head is "This is so fucked up." I'm filled with rage toward everyone who allows things like this to happen, and ideas about what people should do to prevent them. However, when I'm lost in indignation, I'm blind to the fact that I'm suffering. Unaware of my own pain, it controls me and eats away at my humanity. So many of us are suffering, and our suffering is dominating our lives because we don't realize it's there. If we don't know we're in pain, there's no way to handle that pain skillfully.

This pattern happens all the time in interpersonal conflicts too. If you're arguing politics with your aunt, you're most likely thinking about why she's wrong. You're probably less aware of the frustration and alienation you're feeling. From that state there's almost no chance that you'll find a shared understanding.

If we don't want to keep being hijacked by our suffering, we need to start by recognizing when it's present. Only if we're aware that we're suffering do we have any hope of being able to respond effectively. So we train ourselves to pay attention to the physical sensations in our bodies, moment by moment.

Most of us don't notice whether we're angry, sad, or scared until the intensity of that feeling is, like, an 8 out of 10. By that time, our suffering has completely taken over. Sometimes we can't even name what we're feeling until we've already caused significant damage. We look around at the smoldering ashes and say, "Wow, I must have been pretty mad." However, it's possible to learn how to notice our suffering when it's still small. If your fear is a 3 out of 10, it's much easier to respond skillfully.

## RADICAL ACCEPTANCE

Sometimes you can tell yourself, "Don't be frustrated," and the frustration just goes away. However, a lot of the time it's not that easy. If you notice that suffering is present in you, and just telling yourself not to feel bad doesn't work, it can be incredibly helpful to *come home* to the present moment and practice radical acceptance of what you're feeling.

In the context of learning how to be present with our suffering, radical acceptance means something very specific. It doesn't mean that you should accept social injustice, violence, or whatever external problem that's triggering you. You might end up feeling differently about the problem as a side effect of this practice, but it's not the place to start. It also doesn't mean you should blindly accept whatever story you're telling yourself about the problem, because our stories are often wrong. Instead, we begin the practice of radical acceptance by focusing on the sensations in the body, because "my chest feels tight and my whole face is tense" is something you can know for sure, while "that guy is an asshole" is just an opinion.

When you notice that you're suffering, bring your attention to the sensations in your body. Bodily sensations are your anchor to keep you from being thrown around by the storm of your emotions. In a moment of suffering, your thoughts will move quickly, and it takes a huge amount of training to be able to watch those thoughts without getting carried away. Instead, it's much easier to come home to your body.

Thich Nhat Hanh tells a story about a time he went for a walk in the summer in France. He was staying at his hermitage in Plum Village, the monastery he founded near Bordeaux after being exiled from Vietnam. It was a beautiful, warm day, and he had all of his windows open. After practicing some calligraphy, he decided to go for a walk in the rolling hills. He wandered through the forest and fields of sunflowers until a freak thunderstorm hit without warning. By the time he made it back to his hermitage, his desk was soaked and the wind had blown ink and paper all over the floor. When he saw that his room was trashed, the first thing he did was to close the windows. With the windows closed, he then cleaned up his space.

If we come home to our mind and body and find that our place is trashed, the first thing to do is to close the windows of our senses. Stop taking in new sights and sounds so that we can focus on what's happening inside. Then we can begin the practice of cleaning up—the practice of caring for our suffering.

A lot of us treat our feelings like my friend Bruce treated his college dorm. By halfway through the first semester of freshman year, his room was so disgusting that he avoided going in whenever he could. Eventually he started sleeping on the couch in the common room. When you keep choosing to distract yourself, stay busy, and avoid being alone with your feelings, you end up like Bruce—incapable of feeling at home in yourself.

When I first began the practice of coming home and paying attention to my mind and body, what I encountered resembled a bomb going off in a shit factory. I was a mess. I had been avoiding my feelings for my entire life, and beginning to pay attention to them was not a pleasant experience. But I'm so thankful that I kept at it. I now know what it feels like to be comfortable in my own skin, and I'm able to stay human while dealing with some pretty hard situations. Really, I believe that just about everything good in my life comes from my commitment to this practice—my willingness to come home to myself, especially when I feel terrible, and give myself complete acceptance.

Let me describe how this practice works in just a few words, and then I'll answer questions.

## PRACTICE

- Notice that suffering is present in you.
- Focus your attention on the physical sensations in your body. Name what you notice, like tension in your face, relaxation in your abdomen, heaviness in your chest, agitation in your whole body, and so on.
- Allow those sensations to do whatever they want to do. They can get stronger, change, or stay the same. Your only job is to feel them—to keep paying attention with open acceptance.

When you start this practice, a few different things might happen. You pay attention to the sensations in your body, and then feel them without trying to change them at all. Whatever distress was there might begin to fade. If it does, that's great. However, it could also stay the same or even get stronger. When that happens, try to remember that this practice isn't actually about trying to make our distress go away. Instead, we're learning how to tolerate and accept whatever feelings arise in us, whether they're pleasant, unpleasant, or neutral.

## What is this supposed to do? Why would that help?

The simplest reason it helps is that hating our suffering and fighting against it will inevitably just make it worse. We become afraid of our fear, we hate our anger, or we get depressed about how depressed we feel. If I'm already suffering about some shitty things in my life or the world, it's got to be obvious that hating myself won't make anything better.

So this practice is about learning a different way to respond to our suffering—one that can actually help. This practice is radical acceptance of our feelings in the body. It's about developing a very specific way of paying attention to our suffering that can create real transformation.

The best analogy I know for illustrating the exact kind of presence that transforms suffering is how we hold a crying baby. I don't mean the way we hold a crying baby at 3:00 a.m. when we're sleep deprived and burned out. I mean instead that there's a way to hold a crying baby that the baby finds comforting. On the other hand, when you hold a crying baby and you're like, "I can't handle this. Please shut up," the baby isn't likely to experience that as particularly soothing.

So you hold the baby, with radical acceptance. You say, "It's okay for you to feel whatever you feel. It's okay for you to cry, or to stop crying. I totally accept you either way." This is the equanimity that is open to whatever might arise. At the same time, you want to help in any way you can. There is care, compassion, and warmth. The words to express this part might be, "I'm here for you. I want to help if I can."

When we think about our relationships with other adults, it can be hard to imagine having both acceptance and compassion. We believe that accepting someone means we don't want them to change, and trying to help someone feel better means that we don't accept their pain. Frankly, that's bullshit. The way that we hold a crying baby is the archetype of *compassion with equanimity*. It's the exact kind of presence that transforms suffering, and the kind of presence we're training ourselves to develop in this practice.

The late, great neuroscientist Jaak Panksepp discovered that every mammal has a well-defined anatomical structure in its brain that governs expressions of care. He called it the Care Circuit, and when it's active, it releases oxytocin and natural opiates to give us that warm, fuzzy feeling. In fact, whenever you're feeling tenderness and love, if we could image your brain with enough detail we'd see that your Care Circuit is active. Panksepp showed that activating the Care Circuit in any mammal (either naturally or using microelectrodes) radically reduces that mammal's experience of distress. In other words, learning how to practice loving and radical acceptance toward our suffering is a direct way to make use of one of our brain's core structures for regulating distress.

**Sorry, but I'm still not clear on "compassion with equanimity." Can you explain a little more?**

Sure. If each time you hear about something bad happening, you're overcome with concern—if it hurts you so deeply that it doesn't feel sustainable—we could call that *compassion without equanimity*. On the other hand, if you hear the same news story and you think, "Yeah, that happens a thousand times a day," and you don't feel particularly motivated to help in any way, that could be called *equanimity without compassion*.

I'm saying that it's possible to develop *compassion with equanimity*. We can train ourselves in the ability to care deeply without being harmed by doing so. In my experience, the best way to develop this quality is by practicing it in relation to our own suffering. We learn how to hold our suffering—our fear, grief, or anger—like we'd hold a crying baby. Once we can relate to our own pain in this way, everything else gets easier. We become able to care deeply about other people's pain without it feeling debilitating. This skill allows us to be so much more helpful in the world.

**What if the feeling is way too intense? What if it's traumatic?**

We all have a finite capacity for being present with suffering. If the suffering is too big, we'll get overwhelmed. If the pain in you is too intense for you to be able to hold it with compassion, you need to be careful because it's possible to make things worse.

Bringing up pain and holding it with compassion leads to transformation. Bringing up pain without compassion is ruminating, and it will make the pain grow. It's important to know your limitations and get support. For a beginner, it's never a good idea to practice with acute trauma on your own (yet, I can say from personal experience that it's possible to practice with trauma once you have enough training and guidance).

It's okay if the feelings that come up for you are really unpleasant. You might have much more capacity to embrace your pain than you ever knew. The way to know if your suffering is too intense to practice with on your own comes down to whether you feel like you're able to hold the feeling with loving presence, or if you're just being tortured by it.

This is a really important topic, so you can jump to chapter 8—"Healing Old Pain"—to get more detailed guidance.

### What if I can't stop thinking?

You try to come home to your body and pay attention to all the sensations you find there, but you get carried away by thoughts, memories, and commentary. That's totally normal and should be expected. Here are a few types of thoughts that might come up during your practice, and some instructions on how to deal with them:

- You're telling yourself to accept an unpleasant feeling and the thought pops up, "I hate this feeling. I don't want to accept it."
  - » Label those thoughts *resistance*, because they're resisting your practice. Say to yourself, "This is resistance," and see if it fades on its own.
  - » If it doesn't, make it the object of your compassion and acceptance. Empathize with this voice in you. Try saying something like, "Of course you hate this feeling. That's totally natural." Then see if you can allow both the sensation and the voice that hates the sensation to be present in you at the same time. They're both already there, so let them be. Don't pick sides. "I allow myself to feel the tension in me, and I allow the voice that hates this tension to say whatever it wants. I'm open to both."
- You're trying to practice and you think, "This practice isn't helping. I'm terrible at this."
  - » Label those thoughts *doubt,* because they're doubting the effectiveness of your practice. Say to yourself, "This is doubt," and see if it fades on its own.
  - » If it doesn't, try to empathize with this voice, too, but do your best to remain agnostic. Try saying, "There's a part of me that believes the practice isn't working. That might or might not be true. It's perfectly okay to feel like that." Allow that voice to say whatever it wants and keep coming back to the sensations in your body. Sometimes

doubt is telling us that we should shift something about how we're practicing, so it's helpful to follow its advice. However, often it's just our insecurities, and what it needs is love.

- You're trying to practice and you think, "I need to buy dish soap."
  » Label these thoughts *planning*. Say to yourself, "This is planning," and see if it fades on its own.
  » If not, this could be your mind making sure you don't forget something important, or it could be an attempt to avoid uncomfortable feelings. If you're worried you'll forget something, you can pause your practice and write it down. Otherwise, try to persist in coming home to the sensations in your body, even if they're unpleasant.
- You get carried away in a story, like, "I know I'm going to get fired" or "I wish she would love me."
  » Label these thoughts *story*, because they're predictions about the future or ways we wish the world were different. Say to yourself, "This is story," and see if it fades on its own.
  » If not, you empathize with this voice, too, but don't agree. "There's a part of me that's scared about something that might or might not be real. I don't need to decide if it's real right now. I can just accept whatever comes up in me." We all have thoughts like this sometimes. Freedom and peace of mind don't come from eradicating them.

They come from learning how to listen to them with radical acceptance and not getting carried away by them.

## Why can't I focus on the emotion? What's special about the body?

I keep saying to focus on sensations in the body, or feelings in the body. All the examples I'm giving are physical sensations—tension, agitation, heaviness, etc. You might wonder why I'm not saying to focus on *fear* or even *suffering*.

The things that we call emotions (fear, surprise, grief, and so on) are characterized a little differently in Buddhist psychology. The simplest way to explain this perspective is to say an emotion such as anger is made of two things: bodily sensations and a tendency to think in a certain way. If I'm feeling angry, the bodily sensations might be tightness or heat in my chest and I might feel my hands balling into fists. At the same time, I have a tendency to think angry thoughts. If you take the emotion called anger, and you subtract the bodily sensations and the tendency to think angry thoughts, there is nothing left. The emotion is entirely made up of those two other things.

Therefore, when you choose to focus on "fear" rather than "tension," you're actually trying to focus on the bodily sensations and the thoughts at the same time. That's harder than just focusing on the body. When thoughts pop up (as they always will), welcome them and come back to the body.

Talking about emotions, naming them, and thinking in those terms are obviously useful in life. I'm not criticizing the idea of emotions. However, I believe this type of practice works better when we focus on physical sensations.

### This is really hard for me. How do I get better at it?

How do we get better at anything? First we learn about it, and then we try it out. Once we've got a feel for it, we practice.

First, this technique has to make sense to you intellectually. If you're blindly going through the motions, it's really likely you'll miss something important. Think about it and read more until you feel like it makes sense. Can you explain why practicing like this would be a useful thing to do?

Then when you're trying it out, don't take yourself too seriously. Instead, experiment with different ways of interpreting these instructions until you find one that feels powerful to you. This is a practice of learning about your mind, so there will always be surprises. Even if you've been practicing for years, be open to the possibility that there's something important you don't yet understand. That openness helps us stay in touch with our actual experience rather than our expectations.

Finally, if you want to be able to respond with compassion in your real life when things are going badly, you have two options. One is to wait for those hard moments and just have the intention to act differently. In this case, you don't think about your practice at all until you really need it. If you choose this path, you'll likely notice some change in five to ten years. The other option is to use practices like this one to train yourself before you really need them. In that way you could see real change in weeks (sometimes days).

The neuroscientist Richard Davidson found that thirty minutes of compassion training a day for two weeks is enough to cause measurable changes in your behavior and brain physiology. If you can't find thirty minutes a day, you can probably find five (either all at once or spread throughout the day). And actually, if you decide that this is really important to you, you might find thirty after all.

The best training for responding differently in moments of suffering is to go to a quiet place and think of something that brings up pain in you. It shouldn't be too intense, but you should feel it in your body. Then practice holding your pain with love and acceptance. This is where the rubber meets the road. The more time and energy you invest in this kind of training, the sooner you'll start to see its impact on you. Eventually you'll find a little more clarity and a little more kindness in a situation that would have previously triggered you. Over time, a painful feeling can become a Pavlovian bell that reminds you to come home to yourself.

### Am I supposed to be doing something with my breathing?

Don't worry about it. If you enjoy focusing on your breath, that's a physical sensation, so it can be part of this practice. But you can also do this without focusing on your breath. Either way, no problem.

### What should I do if this isn't helping?

Try to view this practice as training yourself in the ability to tolerate distressing feelings. It's not about making those feelings go away. Imagine you have a friend who's going through something really hard in her life. She asks you to listen and tells you that she doesn't need advice—just to feel like someone cares. How would you listen to her?

Imagine that you listen to her but the whole time you're thinking, "Okay, I'll listen so that you'll shut up." That wouldn't feel satisfying for either of you. However, if you're able to listen with the attitude of "I want to know what you're going through—I care about your well-being, and I trust your ability to handle this," that's going to feel a lot different, and that's the way we're learning to listen to our own suffering—with openness, genuine care, and faith in ourselves.

Sometimes it can feel like this practice isn't helping because you're not really accepting the suffering in you. You're feeling it and telling yourself to accept it, but it's not authentic. If there's a part of you that hates your suffering, don't pretend it's not there. Acknowledge it and practice acceptance for that part too.

Finally, try to find a way to practice that feels good. The pain we're getting in touch with is obviously unpleasant. But when we succeed at holding it with love and acceptance, there should be at least a little sweetness in the experience. If there isn't, maybe take a break and focus on what's good in your life.

## What if I have chronic pain or a health condition that makes this harder?

There're almost forty years of data demonstrating the effectiveness of mindfulness on chronic pain. For example, we know that eight weeks of training can lead to a 40 to 60 percent decrease in the subjective experience of pain for burn victims. The practice does work.

See if it's possible to feel the sensation of pain in your body without hating it. You could even try to label it *sensation* instead of *pain*. If there's a part of you that's committed to hating it, then welcome that part too. See if you can feel both parts without choosing sides. "I feel this pain in my knee, and the voice in me that hates the pain. I allow both of them to stay or go however they want. I'm here for both of you. I see that you're both suffering and I love you."

We want to be able to face what's fucked up in the world and stay human. The problem is that it hurts to pay attention and care. This practice helps us train ourselves to embrace and transform our own pain, which allow us to stay present even when things are bad.

If there's any limit to the amount of benefit this practice can offer, I don't believe anyone's ever reached it. This practice can take a complete mess like me and turn him into a halfway decent person. But it can also do more than that. The more energy we invest in recognizing and transforming our suffering, the more lightness and connection we find. Personally, I've found that a little dedication leads to a little freedom, and a lot of dedication can radically change your life.

# CHAPTER 4

# KNOW YOURSELF

Holy the supernatural extra brilliant
intelligent kindness of the soul!

—ALLEN GINSBERG

want to propose a hypothesis and we can evaluate it together. The hypothesis is this:

*Everything about you is so amazingly beautiful*
*that you would collapse on your face and sob*
*uncontrollably if you saw it for an instant.*

This is just a hypothesis, so we should examine it in light of all available data. But first, a story:

Victor had been out of prison for about a month when we first met. He was almost seventy years old and had been locked up for forty-eight of those years. His dark eyes were trained squarely on the floor in front of him as he told me that he didn't see a reason to keep living.

When he said that, I felt an immediate, reflexive urge to convince him not to give up. It's hard to listen to anyone who's truly suicidal, because it requires you to face their pain. So instead of listening to him and trying to understand, my first impulse was to argue—to tell him that he was wrong to feel the way he did and that he should look at life differently. Our human desire to avoid suffering at all costs is fucking powerful, and in that moment, mine was trying to steer me away from an authentic encounter with someone in a lot of pain. However, thanks to my teachers and my training I was able to feel that urge but not act on it.

Instead, I told him that I wanted to understand him, and he looked at me with just a little hope in his eyes. He said, "I've wasted my whole life and I'm ready to be done. All I ever did was to hurt people. I've hurt a lot of people, and I hate myself for it. I just don't wanna feel this anymore."

I had no idea what to say or do, so I tried to imagine myself in his shoes. I wanted to find our shared humanity and connect to him from there. I know what it feels like to be full of regret, hopeless, and needing an escape. It feels terrible—like my vital organs are trying to flee from my body, and the last thing in the world I want to do is feel what I'm feeling.

Yet thanks to the brutal absurdity of life, I've learned that feeling what I'm feeling is exactly what I need to do. In fact, whenever we want to escape from a feeling, that's a sign that we must turn ourselves 180 degrees and approach the thing that we desperately want to avoid.

I said, "We're talking, which makes me think that maybe you don't want to hate yourself, but you can't imagine how that could be possible." Now he looked me straight in the face and nodded as his eyes filled with tears.

He said, "I did some really fucked-up things." I thought, "Me too," and I think he could see it on my face because he flashed the faintest hint of a smile. I asked him how old he was when he started getting in trouble, and he told me that he started hanging out with the drug dealers and bullies in his neighborhood when he was about fourteen. "Before that, I was a good kid. I never made trouble."

So I imagined this fourteen-year-old boy who had always been well behaved, and I wondered what led him to get involved with that crowd. I said, "Can you picture yourself as a fourteen-year-old boy? Right around the time you started hanging around those people?" He closed his eyes and nodded again. I asked him what he would say to that boy if he could.

"You think this is fun and you wanna be a big man. That's good. You have dreams. But you don't see where this is gonna take you. You're trying to be big, but you're gonna get locked up in a cage for your whole life! I know! Don't do it. You gotta see where this is taking you. It's not where you think. Look at my life! [He's crying now.] You need someone who can show you how to be big like you want. These people aren't your friends and they're all gonna end up dead or worse. You need a real grown-up who knows about life!"

When he finished, we spent a couple of minutes in silence. Eventually he said, "That feels good, man, but it's too late. It didn't happen." I was struck by how passionate and persuasive he'd been. It was really powerful.

I asked him, "How many fourteen-year-olds are there in your neighborhood who are about to make the same mistakes you did?" He understood immediately, and his expression transformed from pained exasperation to one of focus and purpose.

He said, "That's it. I know something they don't know. They don't wanna hurt anyone. They're just dumb kids. They wanna feel big, but they don't know how. That's it." He was quiet for a minute and then continued, "I couldn't hear what my pain was telling me, man, and it was gonna kill me. It was trying to tell me that I have something important to do, but I couldn't see it. Now I know."

## THE WORST THING ABOUT YOU IS AWESOME

Now I think we're ready to examine our hypothesis: that your every thought, feeling, and action is devastatingly beautiful when seen clearly. But how could we test that? What if I could guide you through a process of examination in which even the worst thing you've ever done looks completely lovable? If we could do that, it would be at least one piece of evidence to support our theory.

Let's try. Think about one of the most fucked-up things you've done in your life—something you regret. Think about something you did that you wish you hadn't, or something you didn't do that you wish you had. Think of the pain you've caused yourself and others.

Once you've chosen something, we're going to look into *why* you did it. Instead of avoiding this uncomfortable part of you, we're going to dig in. What were you hoping for? Were you trying to avoid something bad? Did you believe you were in danger, physically or emotionally? Were you trying to achieve something? Did you think it would feel good or get you something that seemed important at the time? In the moment you made that choice, what was the absolute best-case scenario in your mind?

There is a way of understanding any destructive choice we've made so that its memory transforms from the poison of shame into something that makes us stronger. Whether what you did was a mistake or you deliberately hurt someone, if you can see that choice clearly enough, it will make you more compassionate toward yourself and others, and it will make you a better person.

## SCIENCE AND HUMAN NATURE

This transformative perspective comes from a theory of human nature that's grounded in the most current science. It focuses on two main questions: (1) What motivates us? and (2) How do we translate those motivations into action?

Let's start with the first part. I believe that every thought, feeling, and action is motivated by the desire to avoid suffering and meet needs. In fact, evolutionary psychologists would say it's hard to conceive of any other motivation from a scientific standpoint.

If you try to conceive of evolution being motivated by anything other than avoiding danger and thriving, then it stops making sense. When a moth flies into a candle, we don't think, "That moth hates himself." We think, "Maybe it uses light to navigate and gets really confused by artificial lights." We assume it has a life-serving motivation that gets confused. Entomologists don't actually know why moths do that, by the way. Yet we give them the benefit of the doubt. Why can't we use the same logic when trying to understand our own behavior? Are we that much worse than moths?

I believe that if we knew how to meet all our own needs and make the other people in our lives happy as well, we'd always choose to do that. It's just like how we assume that if the moth knew how to mate and eat and not die, it would do that. The problem is, like Victor said, we're just dumb. And this kind of dumbness seems to be a fundamental consequence of how our brains are designed.

For a long time, the only way scientists could study how the brain works was by observing different sorts of head injuries and how they affect people and animals. Obviously, there's only so much you can learn by this method. Then, when brain-imaging technologies were invented, we could watch which circuits would light up in different circumstances. However, this method is limited too. If you could scan your laptop and watch the electric signals bouncing around, you still wouldn't really understand how it works.

More recently, the fields of artificial intelligence and machine learning have developed to the point that they're making their own major contributions to what we know about the brain. *Computational neuroscientists* create computer models of our theories about the brain and test them to see how those theories behave like real brains.

One of the most prevalent ideas in computational neuroscience is that the brain's primary function is to create models of how the world works. Every living thing has to be able to perceive its environment and respond in some way, even if it's just recognizing food and eating it. Therefore, it has to find patterns in its raw sensory data and translate those patterns into a picture of what's actually happening (e.g., the frog perceives its hunger and the presence of a fly). Most important, it has to have a model of how its actions can impact its world (e.g., snapping my tongue at this precise angle will catch that fly). The model determines how it will act.

How does this translate to human nature? One of the most important aspects of this theory is the idea that our models of the world are *necessarily* made out of the patterns our brains have perceived in our past experience.* In other words, every new experience is interpreted through the lens of our past.

If we combine the basic evolutionary view that behaviors always have some life-serving purpose (although they can get confused) with the idea that the brain is a model-creating machine, we end up with the following picture of human nature: human beings always want to make choices that serve life and lead to the least possible suffering; however, we usually don't know how to do that. Instead, we do the best we can, based on our imperfect models of how the world works.

If you can find a way to see the beauty in that predicament—the beauty in a creature who truly wishes that we could all be happy but has no idea how to make that happen—then compassion begins to arise naturally. Whatever you did that you regret, can you see that you were trying to meet some need? Imagine yourself back in that moment. If you had known a way to meet all of your needs—to avoid whatever discomfort or achieve whatever desire—in a way that wouldn't have hurt anyone, would you have done that instead? If the answer is yes, try saying to yourself, "Just like every other human, I always want to create less suffering and more well-being for everyone in my life. Just like every other human, I don't always know how to do that." How does that feel to say? Can you see the beauty in our imperfections?

---

* It's true that some models are inherited, but we can consider them relevant patterns that our ancestors' brains noticed.

## PUTTING IT INTO PRACTICE

In a hard moment, this perspective can be a lifesaver. As I write this, my wife, Annie, was just released from the hospital after another late-night trip to the ER turned into a weeklong stay. Over the past week, I took care of her in the hospital during the day as she dealt with excruciating physical pain, and then fought traffic to get back to my son, feed him, and put him to bed each night. Every day was an experience of giving all that I can and failing to shield the people I love most from their pain. In short, I had a fucking terrible week.

In this moment, I can feel the trauma in my body. I stop everything I'm trying to do. I stop writing and give myself permission to let go of all my incessant grasping. I stop grasping for happiness, for well-being, for a beautiful book to share with you. I come home to this moment exactly as it is. In this moment, I feel like shit. I'm exhausted, my whole body feels tense, there's a scowl on my face, and I'm way behind in my writing after an unplanned weeklong break. This is it. This is the actual present moment. I don't need to like it. I do need to admit that this is what's real and face it.

My breathing slows and I bring a more focused level of attention to the unpleasant sensations in my body—to the heaviness in my heart and the sick feeling in my gut. With something like courage, I feel them even though I don't want to. I tell myself, "Whatever you feel in this moment is completely okay."

Resistance arises in me immediately—a voice that only wants not to feel like shit anymore.

This is the moment I invoke this theory of human nature. That voice that wants to run away from my suffering, the voice that many meditation instructors would tell you to ignore. I turn my attention completely to that voice and say, "I know that you don't want to suffer. You just want ease and safety. That is the beautiful nature you share with every living thing. I want that for you too. I'm here to help." I mean those words.

The voice in me is soothed, and there's some trust that's built. I return my attention to the suffering in my body, explicitly inviting it to be as strong as it wants to be. I speak directly to my tension, saying, "I see that you're suffering, and I'm here for you. I want to listen to you." My breath continues to get slower and deeper as the tension very slowly begins to dissolve.

Sometimes my mind wanders until the knot of tension in my jaw pulls me back. I return to my practice without any shame about being distracted. Instead, I recognize there is pain in me that needs care and attention, and I recommit myself to providing it. I say to myself, "You wish you could protect the people you love from ever being hurt. That impulse in you is beautiful. You don't have that ability, but you wish you did, so it hurts. I see all of the love in you."

As I recognize the beauty in my pain, it transforms. I feel lighter, and my scowl is gone. I can almost smile. My concentration gets sharper as I focus on each breath and on all of my senses in the present moment. The craving and pain that I embrace become more and more subtle, and my experience of release grows deeper. Eventually my jaw relaxes, my heart feels light, and I once again feel at home in myself. I'm left with a tremendous amount of gratitude for all of the positive conditions in my life.

# CHAPTER 5

# HOW TO STAY HUMAN WHEN OTHER PEOPLE SUCK

For one human being to love another:
that is perhaps the most difficult of all our tasks,
the ultimate, the last test and proof,
the work for which all other work is but preparation.

—RILKE

Human beings, in general, are pretty terrible at getting along with each other. Whether it's two people who are in love but can't stop hurting each other or thousands of people trying to build a social movement but who can't agree on anything, it just seems like it shouldn't be this hard. But it is.

There are a lot of different reasons for this, but many of them can be traced back to the way we're wired to perceive threats. For example, when you're safe and happy, people tend to look pretty nice. However, when you're suffering, especially when you're scared, people fall into one of precisely two categories: (1) those who are doing exactly what you want, and (2) your loathsome and worthless enemies.

In other words, when my bloodstream is filled with cortisol and other distress-signaling hormones, it's really hard to convince me that you're not an asshole, unless you're doing everything I want you to do. When we're triggered like this, it's much harder to resolve a conflict because we're nearly incapable of compromise. Instead, it can often help to prioritize recognizing and transforming our own suffering first. After that, finding solutions gets much easier.

## THE WORST DRUM CIRCLE EVER

During the Occupy Wall Street protests, there was a drum circle happening at one end of Zuccotti Park nearly twenty-four hours a day. I hated that drum circle, and I wasn't the only one. The people who lived in the neighborhood complained constantly about the noise, and people who were trying to hold meetings or discussions in the park could barely hear each other. Still, the drummers refused to stop.

Eventually we held a mediation session at a nearby café. There was a representative from the neighborhood, one from the protest organizers, and one from the drummers. I was asked to be one of two mediators. The representative from the drummers was named Jim, and he explained that many of the people in the drum circle had been homeless in New York for a long time before the protests started and didn't like people coming into their city and telling them what to do.

When a woman representing the neighbors explained that her children were struggling to do their homework because of the drums, Jim screamed at her. He said she was "collateral damage," that she was trying to oppress him, and there was no place for her in the revolution. When the representative from the organizers said he wanted there to be a place for her and that she was part of the 99%, Jim yelled that he didn't care about the 99% and was there for his own revolution.

To me, this exchange is a microcosm of what's fucked up about so many social movements. From a distance, these people seem like they should be natural allies: a homeless man with a revolutionary temperament and a group of people who care deeply about economic inequality. Yet despite all they had in common, they were at each other's throats with the least emotionally stable person dominating the discussion.

As Jim ranted, the other customers in the café started leaving, and it looked like the manager was getting ready to kick us out. I felt like screaming at Jim to shut up, and I had very little hope that this meeting was going to solve anything. I was angry at Jim, afraid that he would derail so many other people's hard work, and I couldn't help seeing him as my adversary.

However, I was supposed to be a mediator. I asked myself, "Can I actually do this or should I tap out and leave?" Frustrated and overwhelmed, I disengaged from the arguing and focused on the sensations in my own body. I recognized immediately the feeling of intense grief in my face and chest. I told myself, "All you want is to help people get along, and that impulse in you is beautiful. You really want these demonstrations to be successful, and you're scared you won't be able to help, so it hurts." I took a minute or so to feel that grief and let go of my attachment to controlling the meeting. I needed to accept that no matter how much I want a specific outcome, it might not happen.

There is nothing defeatist about recognizing that you can't control other people. It's just true. As much as I wanted a successful mediation session, it was looking like it wasn't going to happen. I had been in denial of this fact, and that denial was fueling my anger. After I embraced my suffering, I could see the situation more clearly.

As I welcomed my feelings of helplessness, I began to see Jim differently. His out-of-control behavior had felt like a threat when I was trying to control the meeting. Letting go of that, I saw him as he was: someone who had been treated like shit for a long time. I could see the pain and fear in his eyes, and my heart opened to him.

I looked up at Jim with a very different expression than I'd had earlier in the meeting and said his name quietly. I said, "I don't know about anybody else, but I'm glad you care so deeply about making the world better and about being treated with respect. Whatever we do here, I want us to make sure it starts with making the world better and making sure Jim and the drummers are *fully respected*." Everyone else in the meeting nodded anxiously and looked at Jim. He smiled, and his face resembled that of a scared child, but he nodded too. The tone of the meeting changed, and a week later we had an agreement that the drummers would play for two hours a day at the park and then march around the city for the rest of the day.

## THREE APPROACHES TO CONFLICT

Even though we ended up with a successful resolution, part of me still hates how much time and energy it takes to resolve conflicts. It's a voice in me that sounds like this: "If people weren't so stupid and mean, we could focus on making the world better instead of wasting so much time talking about their bullshit." I imagine most people can relate to that frustration.

However, as annoying as it can be, conflict resolution is incredibly important, mostly because the alternatives are awful. I believe there are essentially three ways to approach conflict: (1) isolation, (2) dominance, and (3) dialogue.

There will never be a relationship that's conflict-free. So when shit comes up, our first option is to leave. I've left lots of jobs, groups, relationships, etc., and I'm usually glad I did. However, if it's the only thing we know how to do in response to conflict, we're going to end up pretty isolated.

The next option is winner-take-all, in which one person dominates and the other submits. Sometimes there's a fight to determine who wins, and sometimes people just fall into their roles—always dominating or always submitting. Either way, handling conflict like this usually means that the winner's needs matter, and the loser's don't.

The third and messiest option is dialogue, in which we approach a conflict with the commitment that *everyone's* needs will matter. We might not be able to figure out how to meet everyone's needs perfectly, but we'll try. For me, the defining feature of dialogue is that (at its best) everyone is on the same side. We are all trying to figure out how to meet the most needs we can. It's not that I'm arguing for my needs and you're arguing for yours. Instead, we're working together to find a solution that meets as many of our *collective needs* as possible.

That might sound unrealistic, but it's not. In fact, with some training, you can learn how to create this kind of connection even with people who are terrible communicators. It's hard and it doesn't always work, but there's a lot more room to improve than most people believe is possible.

## THE TWO POISONS:
## CRITICISM AND DEMAND

When we're in a conflict, most of us stop seeing the humanity in the other person. Instead, they become an obstacle, a tyrant, or a thing that we no longer need. But what if we could stay human—and stay connected—in the middle of a conflict? What if we could see that the other person is trying to avoid suffering and meet their needs just like we are? What if we could value the other person's well-being without *at all dimin-*

*ishing* our commitment to our own? In other words, we would see that both people's needs matter, even if we have no idea how to solve the problem.

To me, this is the essence of dialogue. We won't always meet everyone's needs and we can't solve every problem. However, we can approach conflicts so everyone's needs matter. Therefore, the real goal in conflict is for all sides to value each person's needs equally. If I feel like you value my needs as much as you value yours, then I can tolerate the (likely) possibility that my needs won't get met perfectly.

However, there are two main obstacles—two poisons—that get in the way of this kind of dialogue. They are *criticism* and *demand*. *Criticism* means any negative value judgment about the other person (or oneself). It's a poison when it's unfair, and it's just as bad when it's completely justified. It doesn't matter if your criticism is true, because it will destroy the possibility of real dialogue anyway.

The alternative to giving criticism is not to be a nice dead person without any needs but to recognize that the energy motivating your criticism is an unmet need. Dialogue is possible if you can focus on the need, rather than the fact that the other person is a piece of shit for not already having met it. Real dialogue happens when both people's needs matter. To say that criticism destroys dialogue does not mean we should ignore or minimize our own needs, because that would be submission, not dialogue.

Criticism is sometimes completely justified, but it's also tragic. It's tragic because deep down, every criticism is rooted in this truth: "I hate that you're acting like my needs don't matter." When we express that through a criticism, it usually makes it even less likely that the other person will all of a sudden see the beauty in our needs.

Imagine you did something that a coworker felt was disrespectful. It could have been a misunderstanding or you could have actually been acting like a jerk. It doesn't matter. Imagine how you'd react if they called you an asshole with contempt all over their face. Now imagine that instead they said, "I want to feel like you respect me, but right now I don't. Can you help me understand why you did that?" The second example is expressing the need directly. This doesn't guarantee the other person will react positively, but it definitely makes it more likely.

The other poison to dialogue is *demand*, which means that you're asking for something specific and there will be negative consequences for the other person if they don't do it. Demands are tragic for a different reason. When we ask for something, we'd all prefer that the other person would do it because they want to. If I ask for a ride home from the airport, and my friend rolls his eyes and agrees with a pained expression on his face, that feels kind of shitty. I'd certainly prefer if he brightened up and said, "Awesome. I'm happy to."

When we demand something from another person, we basically make it impossible for them to respond out of joy. They can concede to our pressure or refuse. Either way, with a demand, our preferred outcome won't happen.

Just like criticism, there is an unmet need under every demand. Imagine I said to you, "I've picked you up from the airport three times, and you've never gotten me once." It's obvious I want a ride home, but what am I really hoping for? Deep down, I want you to be happy to get me. However, I'm scared that's not possible. Instead, I believe the only way to get you to help me is to threaten you. "If you don't drive me, then you're a bad person and a bad friend and you'll pay for it."

The way to avoid making demands is to make it as easy as possible for the other person to say "no." For example, I could say, "There are lots of different ways I could get home from the airport, but my favorite would be if you could pick me up." I'm letting you know you have an opportunity to make my life better—that riding with you would be my favorite. It's like saying, "Don't do this because you're afraid I'll judge you if you don't. Do it if it sounds fun."

We're all afraid that other people only do things for us because they're getting something in return or they fear some negative consequence. However, that's not true. The secret to getting other people to enjoy giving to you is to learn to see the beauty in your own needs and theirs. If you believe your needs are burdens, it'll be hard for other people to see them any differently. On the other hand, when you make a request with the confidence that both people's needs are intrinsically valuable, you're much more likely to get the response you want.

So for both of these two poisons—criticism and demand— the key is to recognize that there is always an unmet need underneath them. If you notice yourself making a demand, or you feel like criticizing yourself or someone else, look for the unmet need. Once you find it, try to see its beauty. Then communicate from that insight.

The most powerful example of this process in my own life happened when I proposed marriage to my wife, Annie. We went for a walk around Golden Gate Park's Panhandle, I read her a poem I'd written, and then got down on one knee. When I asked, she responded, "Thanks."

I wasn't sure what "thanks" meant, but after a little discussion it was clear that it didn't mean "yes." It was closer to "not now, maybe later." At that time, we lived together in a two-room trailer at the environmental education center where she worked. Let me tell you that the next several weeks in that trailer were not comfortable.

I was fucking heartbroken. I felt like I'd really put myself out there and gotten rejected. I would constantly ask her what she needed to be clear about on whether she wanted to marry me, but she could never say precisely. The longer this went on, the more adamantly I would plead for some clarity. I'd say, "If you don't know, then please take the time and space to figure it out." I felt desperate and powerless. This went on for about six months. I would press for information, and she would with-draw and equivocate.

Eventually she said, "I feel like the more pressure you put on me, the harder it is to answer your questions. I'd actually like to answer them, but I don't want to feel like I'm doing it because you're forcing me." Hearing that, right in that mo-ment, I was furious. I was in so much pain and all I wanted was some clarity.

From my perspective, I'd been trying to let her know how much her ambiguity was hurting me, but that wasn't how it looked from her side. She was experiencing a demand, and it was destroying our connection. So I took some time to think about how I could express my needs more directly.

The first thing I had to do was figure out what my needs were. So I used this thought experiment: I asked myself what I would do if I had magic powers and could completely control the situation. The answer was that I'd want Annie to tell me her concerns and we'd work them through. Then I asked my-self why that would feel good—like, what needs would it meet? The main one was connection. I'd feel closer to her and safer in our relationship. The clarity would also feel good, but it'd be secondary. Mostly, I wanted to feel safer in our connection.

Now that I was clear about my own needs, I had to find a way to express them that would also respect her need for autonomy. I did my best to say all that to her. It was something like, "I'm scared of losing our relationship, and I don't know how to say that to you in a way where you can still feel free." She responded that she was also really scared about losing the relationship. When I heard that, I felt like screaming, "So just figure out what you need and tell me." It took every ounce of restraint I could muster to keep myself from doing that. I wanted her to see the beauty of my needs and feel the freedom to respond in her own way. So instead I said, "We both really value our relationship, and we're both really scared about losing it." I left it at that. It was the need that was underneath my demand, and I had finally expressed it in a way where both our needs (mine for connection and hers for connection as well as autonomy) were on the table.

Over the next week, I was careful never to tell her what to do. I could finally see the beauty and value in her need for autonomy. I don't want to be in a relationship in which my partner feels manipulated by me (and therefore resents me). I want her to feel completely free to be herself. So whenever I felt insecure, I'd make sure to express that her need for autonomy was just as important to me as my needs for connection and clarity.

By the end of the week, she had expressed three concrete concerns about getting married. We talked openly about them, and decided we'd do it. I did the formal proposal again, and got an actual "yes." I feel so grateful we were able to find a way to value both of our needs.

This story shows how demands and criticism are not just about what the speaker says. They're even more about what the listener hears. There are some people who are such good communicators that they hear the need no matter what we say. I might scream, "Fuck you!" and they respond, "I want you to feel respected. What can I do to help you feel that?" On the other hand, there are also people who only hear criticism and demand no matter what you say to them. You might say, "I'm so glad you could make it to the party," and they say, "I can leave anytime you want."

I feel like most things called "communication techniques" end up being awkward when you use them in real life. However, this one is amazing.

## Best Ever Communication Technique

PART ONE

- Whenever communication is going badly, take a minute and think about whether you're using criticism or demand.
- If you are, think about what unmet need is underneath the criticism or demand. Name it silently for yourself.
- Try to imagine the other person feeling happy to contribute to your need and totally free to do it in their own way.
- Try to express your need directly, without criticism or demand.

PART TWO

- If they are still reacting negatively, say this:
  » "I feel like I'm not expressing myself very clearly. Can you tell me what it sounds like I'm saying?" The trick is that

you say this no matter how clearly you're speaking. It's a way to help the other person feel comfortable telling you what they heard without it sounding condescending.

» They will tell you the criticism or demand they hear. It might be based on a real nonverbal thing they notice from you, or it might be 100 percent their own projection. It doesn't matter.

» You say, "I'm sorry if it sounds like that. I think I'm just doing a bad job expressing myself. What I'm trying to say is [explain your need directly]. Does that sound different? What did you hear that time?"

» Do this until they hear your need without the criticism or demand.

• Seriously. It really works.

**When you say to focus on my own suffering first, do you mean that I have to wait until I'm completely peaceful and enlightened before I bring up a conflict? Because if you do, that's stupid.**

No, I don't mean that stupid thing. I mean something smart. I mean that *sometimes* when we dive headfirst into intense conflict, we end up taking turns punching each other in the face (emotionally speaking). We each have our own limited capacity for tolerating distress, beyond which we're no longer able to do much of anything helpful. Maybe you're really good in explosive conflicts, and you almost never get so triggered that you start indiscriminately throwing chairs at anyone in range (emotionally speaking). If so, that's great.

I'm talking about those of us who *do* get triggered in conflicts and do more damage than necessary. We have to know our own limits, and recognize that there are times it's helpful to disengage temporarily. We don't disengage to punish the other person or to avoid the conflict. We do so to embrace and transform the suffering in our bodies, so we can return to the conflict with a greater capacity to create a positive outcome.

That doesn't mean we have to wait until we're totally peaceful. I don't even know what that would mean. There are Tibetan monks who can get into such deep states of peace that you can shoot a gun next to their heads and they'll have no startle response. I'd have to be an asshole if I thought that were the only state from which resolving conflicts is possible. No, we just get calm enough that we can stay human. Hopefully the practices in this book can help you do that.

My teacher Thich Nhat Hanh taught a practice called *The Peace Treaty*. His advice was that as soon as you realize you're angry, you must tell the other person within twenty-four hours. You tell them, "I'm suffering right now. It has something to do with our relationship, but I don't have enough clarity to know exactly what. I will prioritize practicing with my suffering over the next few days. Once I have some clarity, I'd like to talk with you." I don't always do that, but it works really well when I do.

**I have some really toxic people in my life. Are you saying I have to make them see the beauty in my needs?**

Nope. Leaving relationships is always an option, and sometimes it's way better than trying to dialogue. I also believe there are some circumstances in which the winner-takes-all option (either taking control or giving in) is more practical than dialogue. Having said that, there are times that trying to create dialogue with toxic people can be really rewarding. Nobody is toxic because they're happy. The difficult people in your life act the way they do because they're suffering. Remember, orcs are just tortured elves.

This doesn't excuse their behavior. However, it can create an opening for connection. If I believe the reason someone is doing what they're doing is that they're trying to annoy me, I'm not likely to see their humanity. Instead, if I can see that they're suffering, they want to be happy, but they have no idea how to do that, I might be able to relate to them.

The more destructive someone is acting, the more precious the need they're trying to meet. If someone is screaming and throwing furniture and inventing new curse words, it means the need that's motivating them is vital. They're reacting to something that feels to them like a serious threat to their physical safety or their basic self-worth. If you can reflect that back to them—saying something like, "I can tell you just want to feel understood"—you'll be amazed at how much they can deescalate. I've done this with people in the middle of a psychotic break and still gotten a good response.

**I feel like I don't have enough conflict in my relationship. We just have these big steaming piles of resentment that we don't talk about. Is that a question?**

Sure. Unexpressed criticism and demand are often more toxic than screaming matches. But the practice is the same either way. You recognize and name whatever criticism and demands are present in your relationship (even if they're unspoken). Then you look for the unmet needs that are underneath them. Finally, you express your needs directly and encourage your partner to do the same. Criticism and demand are actually awesome, because they point our attention to the unmet needs we have to address.

**Okay, I tried that. I expressed my needs, and my partner seemed to appreciate them. However, I can tell he has unmet needs that he's refusing to talk about. What about that?**

There's a thing called an *empathy guess*. The first part of it is stating what you observe about your partner in the most objective, value-free way you can. For example, "I feel like you really understand my need for intimacy. But when we talk about it, there's *something about your facial expression* I don't understand." You could describe it, but don't interpret it. You want this part to be a description that's as objective as possible. For example, "You look like you're hiding something" is highly subjective. "Your face looks tense" is better.

The second part of an empathy guess is guessing. Don't act like you know what his need is, even if you're pretty sure that you do, because you might be wrong. You can say something like, "When I see that expression on your face, I wonder if you'd like more freedom and autonomy. Or if there's something else that would make your life better." The great things about an empathy guess is that it orients the other person to thinking in terms of needs, and expresses that their needs matter to you.

It's really common in relationships that one person needs more intimacy and the other person needs more autonomy. When that happens, it can seem scary, like your needs are in conflict. But it's not true. People can have intimacy and autonomy at the same time. Both needs can matter and both can be met. It might be confusing to figure out how to meet both, but 90 percent of the tension goes away as soon as the two of you agree that you both want more intimacy for you and more freedom for him. You don't need to solve the problem right away. The experience of "we both value both people's needs, even if we can't meet them perfectly" is the essence of a connected relationship.

**I have no idea how to guess someone else's need. I don't know what I need. How can I guess my own needs?**

It takes a lot of practice to be able to hear the needs that are underneath criticism and demand. Luckily, the practice can actually be fun. Let's go through a day in the life of your friendly author and pay attention to some of the terrible, awful, no-good thoughts that arise in his mind. Then we'll look for the needs—the living energy—that are motivating them.

- Situation: I'm walking in a hallway and someone is coming from the other direction. I'm on the right side, but the other person doesn't step to my left so we can pass. She steps right at me so I have to stop and stand up against the wall until she passes.
  » Thought: "What the fuck is wrong with you?"
  » Need: "I wish we could share this space and be considerate of each other. I also wish I knew why you did that so I could understand your perspective."

Here's how I did the translation: I imagined myself back in that scene, right as I was criticizing the other person. I didn't try to tell myself not to criticize her or convince myself that she's probably a good person. I asked myself, "What do you wish had happened?" The answer was I wished that she would have noticed me and made space. Then I asked myself, "Why would that feel good? What needs would it meet?" And that's how I got my answers: consideration and understanding. Let's do another one.

- Situation: I'm at a café and I have to take a shit. A guy walks out of the restroom as I walk in and there's piss all over the toilet seat.

» Thought: "FUCK YOU!!!"
» Need: Consideration, respect (not just for me, but also for others in general), and especially understanding. "I wish I knew why you would piss in a public toilet with the seat down, because right now it's hard for me to see you as a human who's trying to create happiness in the world. Did no one care enough to teach you about the consequences of this? Were you afraid of touching the seat? If I could understand how you were trying to meet your needs, I think I wouldn't resent you so much."

Fun, right? Try one yourself. Think about a criticism or demand in your life right now. Who can't you accept as they are? Let yourself get in touch with that brilliant, alive feeling of nonacceptance. Once you have it there, ask yourself, "How do I wish things were different?" It doesn't need to be possible. It can be about how you would change things if you had magic powers. This is just about listening to the need in you. Write down your answer. Then ask, "Why would that feel so good? What needs would it meet?" Now imagine yourself in the situation or relationship and express your needs directly. How does it feel?

# CHAPTER 6

# WHY DO BAD THINGS HAPPEN?

To learn which questions are unanswerable,
and not to answer them: this skill is most needful
in times of stress and darkness.

—URSULA K. LE GUIN

When I was seventeen years old, my mother came into my bedroom with a newspaper clipping and a somber expression. She asked if I knew that I had a half brother. My jaw dropped. Needless to say, I didn't know because she'd never told me. She explained that my father (whom I'd never met) had two other sons, both much older. The newspaper clipping said that my half brother had just lost his license as a surgeon for performing unnecessary operations while on heroin. He was facing manslaughter charges because some of those patients had died.

As you might expect, my seventeen-year-old brain popped. I ran out to my $200 Camaro and drove through Boston side streets at eighty miles per hour to my friend Leon's house. When I got inside and explained to him what had just happened, I was feeling intensely self-destructive. I had no idea what I wanted to do, but I didn't feel particularly attached to living.

Leon listened and was quiet for a while. Then he asked me, "What's this got to do with you?"

I said, "It's my fucking brother! I didn't even know I had a brother, and he's a murderer!"

Leon said, "Okay. So what?"

I was truly shocked that he didn't seem to understand why this would bother me. However, when I tried to explain, I found that I couldn't. Why exactly *did* this hurt so much? None of the stories that ran through my mind really answered Leon's question. I wasn't angry at my mother. More than anything, I felt disgusted with myself, but I couldn't say why.

Leon had suffered. He had family in jail and dead, so it wasn't like he couldn't relate. He was asking how this news directly impacted me—how it changed my life—and I had no answer. Then I realized the thing it actually impacted was my *story* about who I am. If I have a brother who is this fucked up, it must be just a matter of time before I meet the same fate—destroying myself and everyone around me. I'd heard only a few sentences about him, but he completely reminded me of myself. He was really smart (a surgeon), as well as completely fuck-the-world gonzo. That was me, and I felt like I was staring at my own future.

I stumbled through explaining this to Leon, who shrugged and said, "You're not your brother, man." The relief hit me like a tidal wave and I started to cry. He gave me a hug and we spent the rest of the day playing video games.

## THE PROBLEM OF WHY

Why do bad things happen? Why do people do bad things? The stories we create to explain *why* things happen have profound impact on us. They shape how we feel about ourselves, other people, and the world.

For example, there are infinite ways to explain my brother's behavior. Take a second and think about why *you* believe my brother did what he did. Do you think he's evil? Is he sick? Could he be the blameless victim of his conditioning? I'm sure you can imagine someone explaining his behavior in a way that paints him as a worthless, contemptible creature who might be better off dead. You can probably also imagine someone explaining it in a way that would evoke pity for him.

If we want to be able to face what's fucked up in the world and not be destroyed by it—moreover, if we want to have a positive impact—then this question is central. **Why do bad things happen?** Our explanations can make us hate ourselves and others, make us feel powerless, or they can strengthen our capacity to stay human.

There are two parts to this question. The smaller part is psychological. It asks why people do bad things. The bigger part is existential. It asks why bad things happen *at all.*

## The Smaller Part

Let's start with the psychological question. Why do people do bad things?

Before we can begin to put together an explanation for either of these questions, we have to deal with the fact that they aren't the kind of questions that have solid answers. There are countless ways to explain why people act the way they do. If you believe that only one explanation can ultimately be true, then it would make sense that you'd want to figure out which one it is. However, some questions just don't work like that.

There are plenty of theories about human behavior that have major problems. They might be internally inconsistent, or they might be bad at predicting how people actually behave. We don't need to waste time on bad theories. However, there are also a huge number of explanations that are pretty good. They're more or less equally viable, and there's really no way to determine which among them is the one true explanation. There's actually a scientific term to describe this situation. The principle of *underdetermination* means that any given set of data can always be explained in multiple ways.

If we can't know which theory of behavior is the one true theory, then it would make sense for us to adopt one that's helpful—one that makes it easier to relate to people with compassion. I believe the theory of human nature I described in chapter 4 accomplishes this. So to answer our question directly:

- Why do people do bad things?
- Because everyone suffers. Everyone tries to avoid suffering and meet their needs in the best way they can, based on their brain's imperfect models of how the world works. Those models are limited to the patterns their brains perceived in their past experience. In other words, they're trying to create happiness, but they don't know how.

This perspective was articulated beautifully by an activist in Ferguson, Missouri, during the unrest that followed the shooting of Michael Brown. There is a Mexican restaurant right near the police station in Ferguson that kept being damaged and vandalized during protests. At a community meeting, a woman whose family owns that restaurant spoke up, saying, "My family's restaurant keeps getting destroyed. I don't see how any of this violence and rioting is helping anything." A lot of people who were watching Ferguson on the news had similar thoughts.

When she was finished speaking, another woman stood to respond. She had been a community activist in Ferguson for many years and said, "A lot of us have been trying everything we know how to do to stop police violence. We've been working within the system for a long time and nothing made the situation better. If we knew how to stop needless killings in a way that didn't upset anyone, please God, believe we'd do that. I don't know if these protests will create the change we want. However, I do know that going back to filing grievances and working within the system will not. We've tried that road and it led nowhere. This is the first time people have started paying attention to what's happening here, so a lot of us feel like it might be working. I really wish it didn't hurt your family, but I hope you understand."

I'm sure you have some thoughts about this activist's perspective. You might immediately want to argue with her, or you might want to stand up and defend her. You might want to talk with her about other possibilities. This is a perfect opportunity to look underneath the content of what someone is saying to create a real connection.

Agreeing, disagreeing, and educating all have their place. However, they are a million times more effective if they occur *after* you've created a needs-based connection. Take your particular ideas and set them aside for a minute. Now look for your needs and hers. She wants to stop needless police violence, but she isn't sure how. Can you relate? Even if you believe you *do* know how to stop the killings, can you imagine yourself in her shoes? I'm sure you can relate to the way she longs to stop needless violence. I also believe if you knew exactly how to make that happen, you'd have already done it. So before you agree or disagree with her strategy, take a few breaths to remember you both want the same thing but neither of you knows for sure how to accomplish it.

This way of seeing people doesn't automatically turn you into Gandhi. You don't immediately become a Tibetan monk who feels nothing but compassion toward the Chinese soldier who's torturing him. If someone is smashing your windows, there might not be any kind of a reframe that's going to make you feel okay about it, and maybe there shouldn't be.

The value in this way of thinking begins with our intention to stay human in a fucked-up world. We want to be able to look at these kinds of situations without getting so angry or depressed that we can't be helpful. With that intention clearly in mind, we can think of this perspective as a skill we want to develop through deliberate practice. If you want to internalize this way of thinking so it actually changes the way you feel about people, what it takes is training.

## PRACTICE

- Think of something you've done that caused suffering to someone.
- Try to empathize with yourself right in the moment you made that choice. See how you were suffering, and looking for a way out of your suffering. If you had known how to meet your needs without hurting anyone, reflect on whether you would've done that.
- In retrospect, maybe you can see a choice that would have worked better. However, that's no reason to feel ashamed. It means you've learned something since then, which is a good thing.
- Repeat this process for a choice *someone else* has made that has caused suffering.
- The more you practice, the more this perspective will come naturally.

## The Goodness of Suffering

Now for the existential question: Why do bad things happen at all? For me, this question is about how we relate to everything in life that we can't control. The serenity prayer, popularized by twelve-step groups, says:

> *God grant me the serenity to accept the things*
> *I cannot change,*
> *Courage to change the things I can,*
> *And wisdom to know the difference.*

So there are some things in life that we can control (at least to some extent), and a whole lot of shit that we can't. If there's an action we can take to reduce suffering, then we obviously should take it. However, we are also vulnerable to forces over which we have no power.

It's really hard to accept this degree of powerlessness unless we believe that the *"things I cannot change"* are benevolent in some way. If we believe they are completely random, don't give a shit about us, or might actually be hostile toward us, then admitting how powerless we are can be terrifying.

A lot of us try to deny our powerlessness instead of finding a way to make peace with it. When life is going well, instead of feeling gratitude, we convince ourselves that we're the all-powerful one making it happen (these are the Ayn Rand people). When life is shitty, we blame ourselves and make our suffering a thousand times worse. We try to control things that aren't controllable, and it makes us crazy.

At its core, this is also a question of trust vs. mistrust—the very first stage of psychosocial development, according to Erik Erikson. If we can't develop a basic sense of trust toward *what we can't control*, we'll never feel truly safe.

Throughout history, people have struggled with this question: Why do bad things happen? The German philosopher Gottfried Wilhelm Leibniz believed this was one of the most important questions in all of philosophy. He called it the problem of *theodicy*, and as a Christian philosopher he phrased it in a theological form. Leibniz asked: If God is omnipotent and entirely good, why is there evil? When I think about it, I phrase it in more secular ways, such as, How can I feel okay about life given all of the suffering in the world? or, How can I feel a basic sense of safety when there's so little I can control?

When you think about the world as a whole—especially about everything you can't control—you could believe that it's entirely chaotic and random, or you could believe it's governed in some way. If you believe it's governed, you might believe it's governed by a personal God, many gods, or some impersonal underlying force. Further, you could believe that the governing force cares about your individual wellness, or that it doesn't.

If you're hoping (or worried) that I'm going to argue for the best way to think about these questions, I'm not. How you relate to the question of why suffering exists is incredibly personal. Instead, I'll share how I think about it and some of the ideas I find helpful.

The dominant way of relating to this question in Western thought has been to say that there is one omnipotent God who is the author of everything that happens. You don't need to be terrified about the things you can't control, because God is controlling them and He's super nice. As Leibniz points out, however, there are some contradictions in this way of thinking that I believe are best articulated by a headline that appeared in *The Onion*, "God Admits He's Addicted to Killing Babies." A lot of terrible shit happens in the world, and if you believe that there is a God who is authoring it, you have to wonder *why*. That brings us back to our original question: Why do bad things happen?

Many thinkers have responded by saying it's beyond our ability to understand. God killed all those babies (or allowed humans to), he must have a reason, but we don't get to know it. If you can convince yourself to believe this, it can offer a lot of serenity by helping you let go of trying to understand. However, for me, "don't think about it" doesn't always work.

Leibniz himself articulated a perspective that's similar to one found in Tibetan Buddhism. He said that this world must be "the best of all possible worlds." It's similar to the idea in Tibetan Buddhism that the human realm is the best possible realm in which to be born. Tibetan Buddhism speaks of several realms in which someone can be born. There's an animal realm, a hell realm, a human realm, a deva realm, and so on. Of all the realms, the human one is best. Hard to believe? Here's the teaching:

If you're born as a wild animal, your life would be so filled with fear and hunger that you'd have no opportunity to develop spiritually. Verdict: not the best. On the other hand, you could be born in the deva realm, which means you'd get absolutely everything you want as soon as you want it. In the deva realm, all your desires would be instantly fulfilled and you'd never have to deal with powerlessness at all. This is the realm in which pizza and ice cream would be good for you, and everyone would love you in the exact way you want without ever having to be told. Despite how nice this might sound, the teaching says that it's not the best place to be. Being born in the deva realm means you're never given any opportunity to develop anything we might consider a virtue—no patience, no compassion, no resilience, no gratitude. So when your good karma runs out and you leave that realm, it's one of the most painful experiences possible. You can't cope with the loss.

The human realm, by contrast, has *just the right amount of suffering* to constantly encourage us to grow spiritually without completely overwhelming us. I don't relate to this teaching as being about literal rebirth in other realms (and there are plenty of Tibetan Buddhist teachers who don't either). Rather, I believe we all have moments when we're living in a hell realm and moments when life can feel like a deva realm.

The brilliance of this teaching, from my perspective, is that it reminds us of the goodness of suffering. Your ego is constantly telling you that you'd be happier if you lived in a deva realm. In fact, that's basically all that your ego ever does. It says the world would be better if you got everything you want and if nothing bad ever happened. This teaching can help you remember that your ego is wrong. You don't actually want to live in a deva realm because everything you like about yourself comes from having suffered. You might be thinking, "Sure, but we don't need this much suffering." That's a perfectly rational thought. I'll explain a little more, and hopefully it will make more sense.

There's a saying that all compassion comes from having suffered, and that great compassion comes from great suffering. It doesn't mean that all suffering turns into compassion. We wish that were the case, but it's not. It means that all compassion comes from having suffered. If we think about the people in our world whom we associate with great compassion—people like Nelson Mandela, the Dalai Lama, and Thich Nhat Hanh—they're all people who've suffered tremendously. They've been able to utilize that suffering to develop profound compassion.

Thich Nhat Hanh says that we can understand the process of turning suffering into compassion by thinking about how we turn garbage into compost and compost into flowers. Life gives you garbage, but you can learn how to transform that garbage into something valuable. It's not that you try to get rid of the garbage or try not to think about it. Instead, you can recognize its value and transform it into something beautiful. Specifically, we learn how to recognize our suffering as sensation in the body, let go of our stories, and embrace it with compassion.

So when something bad happens—whether it's losing a job or an act of police brutality—there's a folktale that helps me let go of my stories and stay human enough to be helpful. It's about a farmer whose horse ran away. It goes like this:

> *One day, a farmer's horse ran away. All his neighbors came over and said, "What bad luck!" The farmer shrugged and said, "Maybe." A few days later the horse came back and brought two wild horses with it. All the neighbors came back saying, "What good luck!" The farmer said, "Maybe." The farmer's son was trying to saddle one of the wild horses, got thrown, and broke his leg badly. The neighbors came back again, saying, "What bad luck!" The farmer said, "Maybe." Then the army came through town conscripting all the able-bodied young men, and they left his son at home. The neighbors ran back over saying, "What great luck!" The farmer said, "Maybe."*

Even when something has already happened, we can't know the effects it will have in the future. Something that seems terrible today could cause something amazing to happen tomorrow. When I can't imagine any future positive effect that a shitty experience could have, I try to remember that suffering itself can be valuable. It's the compost from which we can grow the flowers of compassion.

When I have control in a situation, it makes sense for me to create whatever outcome I think is going to be best. Hopefully I'm right. But a lot of our suffering comes from agonizing over outcomes we can't control. My mind will label something as *the worst thing that could happen,* and I'll be terrified about it. Those are the moments for me to remember that there's no way to know whether the exact thing I fear could actually be the best possible outcome.

There's a verse in the Tao Te Ching that I find incredibly supportive in my attempts to trust what I can't control. It's the beginning of chapter 29. It goes,

> *Do you think you can take over the universe and improve it? I do not believe it can be done. The universe is sacred. You cannot improve it. If you try to change it, you will ruin it. If you try to hold it, you'll lose it.*

# CHAPTER 7

# THE ART OF NOT EXISTING

All persons, living and dead,
are purely coincidental.
—KURT VONNEGUT

My first meditation retreat with Thich Nhat Hanh was held at a Buddhist monastery in the mountains outside San Diego. I lived and practiced there for three months with hundreds of monks, nuns, and laypeople. Near the end of that retreat, during the morning session as the sun rose over the canyon, Thich Nhat Hanh led us in a practice called Touching the Earth. During one part of that practice, I found myself lying flat on the floor and being asked to visualize how my mother and father are both present in me—how I'm not separate from them.

I could see so much of my mother in me. I could see her positive qualities, such as her assertiveness and concern for justice. I could also see her negative qualities, such as how she isolates from people to avoid feeling too vulnerable. However, I couldn't see any of my father in me, or rather, I refused to. In my mind, I pictured myself as a tree with deep taproots on my left side but no roots at all on my right.

I also knew I was wrong. At the very least, my father's genes are in me. I'm taller and more athletic than anyone in my mother's family, and I know he was tall and athletic. Yet as I lay there, I felt this profound dissonance. One voice in me was saying, "A lot of your physical qualities must have come from your father. Moreover, he's shaped your personality, too, even if just through his absence." The other voice was screaming, "I have nothing to do with him!"

After Touching the Earth was over, I hiked into a ravine and spent the rest of the day in meditation. I sat at the foot of a tree and paid attention to the tension and agitation coming up in my body. With each breath, I welcomed those feelings until I had found enough stillness and clarity to listen to the different voices in my mind. Eventually I got in touch with something dark—a deep and seething hatred that I held for my father.

If you had asked me how I felt about my father just a day earlier, I would have said something like, "It doesn't really bother me. He's never been a part of my life, so it's normal for me." I also believed that I didn't hate anyone. I was so deeply involved in meditation and nonviolent social change that my whole identity was about forgiveness and compassion. So when I realized how much hatred did exist in me, I felt like a huge fraud. It was like, "You believe in all this shit and you act like it's who you are, but underneath, you're still that fucked-up kid from Boston." It felt like this carefully crafted identity I'd built for myself was falling apart. There was no way I could be the person I wanted to be and have this much hatred.

I kept sitting under that tree with my mind reeling. The hate felt like a white-hot poison in me. At that time, I believed that hatred itself was the thing that was destroying our world. Hatred was the bad guy. Even Thich Nhat Hanh had called it "the enemy of Man" in his famous letter to Martin Luther King Jr. I'd been trying so hard to be one of the good guys, but I was beginning to fear that it wasn't going to be possible. I thought maybe people don't really change.

Then my mind returned to the practice of Touching the Earth. In that practice, we're guided to see every part of ourselves—every physical and psychological quality—as *not me* and *not mine*. Instead, they're called *nonself elements* that have been transmitted to us in various ways. In other words, everything I love about myself and everything I hate about myself didn't come from nowhere. I didn't cause myself to be tall or to love books. I didn't cause this hatred in me, and it didn't originate with me. Everything comes from somewhere. Maybe if I could see the hatred as a transmission instead of identifying with it, I wouldn't feel so ashamed.

I focused my attention on the hatred in me. Despite every fiber of my being wanting to escape and avoid that feeling, I stayed with it. I allowed all of my internal alarm bells to freak out. My jaw tightened, my skin crawled, and I felt intense heat in my chest, but I didn't fight any of those feelings. I just kept whispering to myself, "Whatever you feel is okay. I'm here for you." Eventually my body settled and I had enough presence of mind to explore the hatred itself.

As I was taught in Touching the Earth practice, I looked for the conditions that had caused this feeling in me. The hatred was a response to my father, so I looked to see how he might be present in it. I recognized that his absence in my life, how he'd avoided all my attempts to contact him, and all the shitty things I'd heard about him were manifestations of his suffering. The suffering in him had caused him to hurt other people. When that happened, it's like his suffering was being directly transmitted to them—to me. I saw the hatred in me as the portion of my father's suffering that he'd transmitted to me. He'd given me his height, his build, and his pain.

I could see the hatred wasn't *me* and wasn't even really *mine*. It was made out of suffering that existed before I was born, and as I looked deeper, it was clear that it hadn't originated with my father either. I know very little about his background, but it's easy to assume that he wasn't raised with abundant emotional support and secure attachment. As my understanding shifted, the hate in me no longer felt like a damning indictment of who I *really am*. The hate was made of suffering, and the suffering was part of an intergenerational transmission. It was present in me, but I began to feel like its steward or caretaker rather than being defined by it.

As I sat in the ravine, my insight slowly ripened. "The hate in me is the continuation of my father's suffering. If I do nothing about it, I'll transmit this suffering to everyone in my life and to future generations. However, if I can find a way to heal and transform it, I can leave the world a little better than I found it." At the time, my practice wasn't strong enough for me to hold all that pain with compassion, but I decided that's what I wanted to do with my life. I wanted to learn how to embrace and transform even the most intense suffering, and help others develop that skill too.

## THE CLOUD IN YOUR TEA

In Buddhism, we learn about the teaching of nonself. It's complicated, subtle, and really easy to misunderstand. However, when you apply it correctly, the result is that you feel freer, more connected, and more fully alive. Maybe most important, at least in terms of staying human in a fucked-up world, it's a teaching that can help you not to feel ashamed of your suffering or unskillfulness, and it can help you let go of your attachment (or aversion?) to praise.

Everything you hate about yourself *isn't you*, so don't worry about it. Everything you love about yourself *isn't you*, so don't feel too proud. They're all nonself elements. They're transmissions from past generations. They're entirely made out of things that aren't you. You don't even exist, at least not in the way you usually think.

Here's how the practice of nonself works: we'll choose something and then apply a special kind of analysis. We'll start with tea and then progress to human beings.

Pour yourself a cup of tea and hold it in your hands. Take a moment to look at it. Let your body and mind relax. Can you see that there's a cloud floating in your cup? Look deeply.

Where did this water come from? From your tap. Farther back, from a reservoir. And before the reservoir, it was rain. Before that, it was a cloud in the sky. Each molecule of $H_2O$ in your cup has been $H_2O$ for millions of years and longer. It has been part of every ocean and floated as vapor above every continent. It's been the blood of countless animals. For the moment, it's your tea. Soon it will be *your* blood. Before long, it'll continue its journey and know every ocean again. Can you see that?

You might believe this tea used to be a cloud, but it isn't anymore. That's the idea I want to deconstruct now. I want to help you see that the cloud isn't gone. In our normal way of thinking, which Buddhists call *sakkaya ditthi* (self view, as opposed to nonself view), every object has a separate self. For example, I am separate from you, and the table is separate from the floor. In this view, each object exists independently of everything else. It has its own separate self. However, I want you to look at the tea differently.

The existence of the tea in your cup is not independent. It depends on many factors. If the cloud hadn't existed, this tea couldn't exist. Since the tea's existence is dependent on the cloud's, they can't be truly separate, and the cloud is not really gone. More precisely, the tea is the continuation of the cloud. The cloud is called a *nonself element*, and the tea is made of many such elements. Without the farmers and truckers who grew and brought your tea leaves (and all their ancestors), the tea wouldn't be here. Its heat came from natural gas in your stove, which comes from prehistoric plankton that absorbed heat and light from the sun. Looking into your tea, can you see all of the nonself elements that are present? They are incalculable. Try to see your tea's existence as the continuation of these elements.

Finally, this teaching states that if you take away all of the nonself elements that make up your tea—the cloud, the farmer, the plankton, etc.—there is absolutely nothing left. The tea has no essential "self" that remains when its nonself elements are removed. In fact, it can be understood to be the unique intersection of all these factors. I'm trying to describe a way of looking at your tea that will make your experience more beautiful and mysterious. If it doesn't feel like that—if these words haven't conveyed that understanding—don't worry about it. It might make sense later.

However, if you can see that your tea is entirely made of nonself elements, then you're ready to look at yourself in the same way. One traditional way of practicing with this teaching is to think about five factors that constitute a human being:

(1) physical body, (2) feelings, (3) perceptions, (4) thoughts, and (5) awareness.* We analyze each of these factors to see that they're made entirely out of nonself elements, and then see how that perspective changes the way we feel about ourselves.

Start with your body, and see how it's entirely made out of elements that aren't your body. Every atom in your body has a history that begins long before you were born. Each came to your body as food, drink, or the air you breathe. Those atoms are shaped by the genes you've received from your ancestors, conditioning from your society, and so on. They're also shaped by your feelings, perceptions, thoughts, and awareness. If you try to take away all the nonbody elements, there's nothing left of your body. Your body isn't *you* or even really *yours*. It's the coming together of these countless elements.

When we see our bodies from this perspective, we don't feel so proud of the parts we like, or so embarrassed about the parts we don't. Instead, your body becomes a unique, precious, and ephemeral gift. Try it for yourself.

You can apply the same analysis to your feelings, perceptions, thoughts, and awareness. For example, what would be left of your thoughts if we took away the thoughts of everyone you've ever known, and then took away your body, feelings, perceptions, and so on?

---

* To clarify the last three: *perceptions* means your experience of your five senses; *thoughts* are the narratives your mind creates out of those perceptions; *awareness* is the subjectivity that is conscious of your perceptions and thoughts.

As you recognize how these five factors are made of nonself elements, they no longer define you, and you can appreciate their beauty. ***This is the art of not existing.*** It's not some kind of nihilism or denial of our common sense. It's a perspective that allows us to relate to our body, feelings, thoughts, etc., as transmissions that we steward for a while, and then release. We see ourselves as part of a stream of life that has existed and will exist for geological time at least.

Do I believe this is the only true perspective? No. I believe the teaching of nonself is intellectually robust, but so are plenty of other worldviews. For me, its value comes from the freedom and well-being it can provide when properly understood.

## THE INTERGENERATIONAL CONVEYOR BELT OF SHIT

We all need a myth to live by. We need some orienting story to help us make sense of the chaos of our lives. Having a myth is completely rational and is in no way opposed to a scientific worldview. I love science. I love science so much that I have a tattoo on my shoulder with the word *science* in a heart,[*] and it really bothers me that so many people believe myths are the opposite of science—as in myth vs. fact. The purpose of a myth is not that it's true. The human mind thinks in terms of stories,

---

[*] Not kidding.

and the purpose of a myth is to help us orient our lives around whatever we believe is truly important.

One of the core myths in my life is the idea that every human being is a worker in a factory that produces the complex beauty of life. We all stand along a conveyor belt and receive transmissions from past generations. As a worker in this factory, we each have two jobs: to appreciate everything beautiful that has been passed on to us, and to transform the suffering of past generations. If we can transform even a little bit of this ancestral suffering, we'll leave the world better than we found it, which (for me) is the highest measure of a human life.

Sometimes the conveyor belt offers us an exquisitely beautiful flower, and when that happens our only job is to allow it to bring us joy. We just have to notice its beauty, and pay attention. If we do, the flower will be strengthened and so will we. However, if we get too proud that the conveyor belt brought us a flower and start looking around to see how much better it is than what other people are getting, we'll miss the opportunity to appreciate it. It'll fly by without really enriching our lives. Without our attention, the flower will begin to wilt.

On the other hand, a lot of the time, the conveyor belt brings us a big steaming pile of shit. It's the suffering of past generations arriving in our lives, completely uninvited. When it shows up, we're each holding a magic wand made out of compassion. Our job when we're given a pile of shit is not to turn away but to touch it with our wand of compassion so that it's transformed.

This work is not pleasant. It requires a willingness to be up close and personal with other people's shit. However, there's nothing that could be more important. We get a pile of shit. We touch it with compassion and let it go. Another pile of shit, and we do it again. The amazing part is that when you touch a pile of shit with compassion, it becomes compost. In future generations, that compost will have the ability to grow a flower—to become a source of joy. Suffering, when met with compassion, can become wisdom, which leads to joy.

However, sometimes it's just too much. It's just pile of shit after pile of shit, and they're not even normal-looking. They look diseased or something, and we're like, "What the fuck? Is it just me that's getting all of this? Why is this happening? Is something broken?" And as we're freaking out, all that shit is passing us on the conveyor belt and heading toward future generations.

The purpose of this myth is to illustrate a subtle point. We don't need to feel ashamed about the ways that we hurt ourselves and other people. Every human being receives a share of this ancestral suffering, and every human being passes some of it along. You didn't create any of the pain in your life out of nothing. When we see that our suffering is made of nonself elements, it can't define us. However, there is something that each of us can do to transform at least a little of the suffering we've been given. We can learn to embrace it with compassion and acceptance.

CHAPTER 8

# HEALING OLD PAIN

You wanna fly,
you got to give up the shit
that weighs you down.

—TONI MORRISON

John Dunne is one of my top ten favorite living philosophers. Possibly top five. He was on a panel and was asked how Buddhism conceives of justice. He responded by dropping his pen on the floor and asking if it "deserved to fall." When someone does something shitty, we think about what kind of punishment they *deserve*. Do you deserve love, or do you deserve the suffering in your life?

Dunne explained that Buddhist philosophy doesn't really concern itself with what anyone deserves. It's concerned with what actually happens, why it happens, and how we can act to create less suffering in the world.

What if we stopped caring about what people deserve? What if we stopped thinking in terms of what *should* happen, as opposed to what *did* happen? What if we completely replaced our concept of justice with the question of how to create less suffering in the world? Think about this Venn diagram:

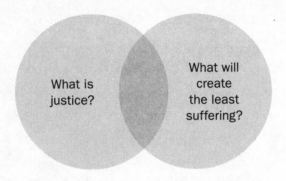

I believe everything valuable about the concepts of justice, what we *deserve*, and what *should* happen are contained in the question of what will create the least suffering (such as how to share resources, keep people safe, and so on). On the other hand, almost all of what's considered "justice" but isn't about minimizing suffering has to do with revenge, retribution, and other stupid bullshit that helps exactly no one. This shift in thinking is particularly important when we're talking about how to respond to perpetrators of violence, such as the person in my next story.

Jared grew up in Indiana,* part of a particularly unforgiving Evangelical church. When he came to see me, he spoke about the depth of his self-hatred and shame. He was socially isolated and often thought about harming himself. When Jared was seven years old, he molested his five-year-old sister.

---

* All identifying details have been changed in this story.

What comes next is a story about healing. It's a story about turning shame into regret, and regret into an active commitment to protect children. But before I go into Jared's story any further, we need to deal with the fact that a lot of people don't want to hear Jared's story. Some people believe Jared *deserves* to hate himself, and to suffer as much as possible. They believe that any healing would mean he gets away with his crimes. Other people might be okay with the idea of Jared healing, but they don't want to hear about it. They ask, "Why don't you tell his sister's story?" I've certainly worked with a lot more people who would be considered the blameless victims of trauma than I've worked with the perpetrators.

I want to tell Jared's story precisely because it's hard to hear. As soon as we recognize that suffering is collective, it becomes so obvious that torturing a perpetrator in prison will only make them more likely to harm someone again. They'll transmit their suffering to everyone unlucky enough to cross their path.

Our suffering is collective, and our healing is collective. Maybe people are scared of this idea because they believe healing is some kind of soporific that makes you feel nothing. However, real healing doesn't erase regret. It turns pain into compassion and makes us more sensitive to our impact on others. Actual healing makes us motivated to be of service. Here's what it looks like:

When Jared approached me for a private consultation

during a meditation retreat in Chicago, he was on the verge of tears. He said, "I did something really terrible, and I've hated myself ever since. Is it possible to find any peace if you've done something like that?" I responded that it's always possible to transform suffering, but it takes dedication. Then I asked if he was willing to tell me what he did. He did, and I told him I could help him but that it wasn't going to be easy. He said, "I'll do whatever it takes."

We sat in silence for a minute or so. Then I guided him to close his eyes and focus his attention on the sensations in his body. I asked what he felt and he said, "I just want to die."

I responded, "I understand. There's a voice in you saying you want to die, and that's okay. We don't need to make that voice go away right now." I took a deep breath and continued, "While that voice is there, what do you feel in your *body*? Is there tension, agitation, or anything like that?"

With his eyes still closed, he said, "It feels fucking awful. Like sick to my stomach, and my face is really tense. I just want to disappear."

"Okay, that's perfect," I reassured him. "Now see if you can allow yourself to feel all of this without trying to make it go away. It might feel terrible, but just for a few seconds, see if you can stay with it. The feelings might get stronger; they might stay the same or change. What do you notice now?"

"It's the same. It's not changing, and I don't want to feel it anymore."

"That's perfect," I said. "There's a voice in you that doesn't want to feel this anymore. The sensations are there—the sick feeling, the tension—and that voice that hates those feelings is there. See if you can allow them both to be there. They're both already there, and you're just allowing them to be. What do you notice now?"

Jared said, "Yeah. It calms down a little." His eyes remained closed as his face softened and his breathing slowed.

I guided him to continue this practice for a few more minutes, bringing radical acceptance to his body and mind. When he seemed relatively calm, I asked him to picture himself as a seven-year-old boy, and then I asked if that boy looked happy or sad.

"He looks nervous, like worried. I also know he's really lonely."

I said, "Okay. As you see him there, what do you feel like saying to him?"

Jared said, "I fucking hate what you did."

"Good," I said in a soothing tone. "Can you tell the boy *why* you hate what he did?"

"Because you hurt your sister and you're supposed to protect her," he said with rage in his voice.

I paused for a moment and said, "Yeah, tell him that you never want his sister to be hurt. Then ask him if he was trying to hurt her."

"I don't want your sister to be hurt!" he nearly screamed,

and then broke down into tears as he asked, "Did you mean to hurt her?"

"What does he say?" I asked.

"He cries and says he didn't know. He thought they were playing."

"Okay. I want you to say that back to him. Say, 'You thought you were playing, but you hurt your sister very much. She's going to feel really bad about it for a long time.' Say that and let me know how he responds."

Jared answered, "He cries and says he's so sorry. But what's the point of this? It doesn't fix anything. The damage is still done."

"That's true." I pause and continue, "Now look at this seven-year-old boy. He's crying and feeling terrible about the damage he's done. He didn't mean to hurt anyone, but he has. He's just now starting to see how much suffering he's caused. I want you to see that—see his pain and regret. Take as long as you need, but whenever you feel moved to say something to him, say it."

Jared was quiet for a long time. Finally he said, "Fuck! I just wish it didn't happen."

I suggested, "Try saying to the boy that you *both* wish it didn't happen." He did and nodded, indicating that it rang true. Then I continued, "Now try saying to him that you know he wouldn't have done it if he'd known how much it would hurt his sister. Let me know if it feels true to say that."

Jared didn't answer. Instead, he began sobbing uncontrollably. Eventually he said, "I want to hate him, but he's just a kid." He cried for a long time, and eventually looked up at me and said, "This isn't working. I feel worse. It's like the hate isn't there anymore, but I feel so fucking sad."

"This is grief," I said. "You're beginning to truly grieve. Come back to your body for a moment, and let me know what sensations are there. Is it tense, heavy, or something like that?"

"It's like a huge weight on my chest."

"Okay," I said. "See if you can let it be there. Try saying to the weight, 'You can be as heavy as you want to be. I can hold you. I'm here for you.' Notice that it's not crushing you."

He nodded and was quiet for a long time. Every couple of minutes, I'd remind him to stay with the weight on his chest—to feel it. Finally he opened his eyes and looked completely exhausted. He said, "I can't handle feeling all of this and being powerless to fix anything." I empathized with him, but affirmed that he might not be as powerless as he feels. After a few more minutes of feeling his grief, we talked about actions he could take to keep children safe from sexual abuse. We finally ran out of time, so he thanked me and left.

That was the last time I saw Jared, but I get emails from him sporadically. He now volunteers as an advocate and educator against childhood sexual abuse. He even shares his story with parents to talk about strategies for keeping kids safe. He told me that every time he tells his story to a group of parents, he imagines that he just saved one child. He also continues to practice feeling his grief. He says it's become more tolerable, but he isn't sure it'll ever go away.

Okay, now let's take a breath. That was an intense story.

Not every perpetrator of sexual violence is capable of this kind of transformation, and certainly not so quickly or directly. There is also some evidence that true sociopaths exist—people who might be neurologically incapable of empathy.* However, many more people are capable of healing than get the chance to. Americans in particular are really good at throwing people in the garbage can, and I hope this story can exert a moderating influence on that tendency in us.

When I share Jared's story, some people feel triggered by it. Others—particularly if they've hurt someone in the past and hated themselves for it—tend to feel relieved. Whatever you're feeling right now, you can learn from it. You can apply it toward your greater purpose. We want to stay human in a fucked-up world. Yet the pain and trauma we carry from the past can make that feel impossible. Old pain can make us perceive threats where there are none, activating the threat-response system in our brains and bodies. It can take us out of the present, closing our hearts and minds.

Jared's story is an example of what I mean by healing pain from the past. Healing doesn't make us feel happy about the

---

* Research suggests they're disproportionately in prison or in positions of power in finance and government.

ways we've hurt people. And it doesn't make us happy about the ways that other people have hurt us. It doesn't make us stupid and it doesn't make us forget. Instead, healing brings us into the present. We stop living in a world that's defined by our trauma, and we enter a world in which our pain is just one part of our life story. Healing helps us prevent future traumas because we develop the ability to discern the difference between safety and danger, rather than seeing danger everywhere. Most important, healing allows us to more fully experience safety, joy, and love when they're present.

## THE HUNDRED-YEAR-OLD TREE

If you imagine a hundred-year-old tree, it's pretty clear that the fifty-year-old tree is concretely present inside it. You can count the rings and point to the fifty- or the twenty-year-old tree. The tree's past is never really gone.

Humans are similar in the sense that our past experiences are stored in the connections of the neural networks in our brains. For example, if a dog bit you when you were eight years old, new connections were made in your brain at that time, because that's how our brains store information. If you are still affected by that experience in any way, some of those connections must still be present, like the rings in a tree.

We can't change the past, but we can change how those memories are stored in our brains. The term that neuroscientists use to describe this process is *memory reconsolidation*. Our memories are constantly being overwritten and changed based on new experiences. This is a well-studied phenomenon.* It's the reason why if you witness a crime, you're told not to talk about it until you're deposed, and they want to depose you as soon as possible. We know that every time you talk about what you saw (and actually every time you think about it), the memory itself is changing.

Put very simply, whenever you activate a memory, it enters a state that neuroscientists call *labile*, or changeable. In that state, it can make new connections with whatever is happening in the present. When Jaak Panksepp spoke about memory reconsolidation, he emphasized how it affects emotional memories. He demonstrated in laboratory studies that any time a mammal—a rat, monkey, or human—recalls a distressing memory, if you can activate the Care Circuit** in its brain, a new association develops. When that memory is put back into long-term memory (i.e., reconsolidated), it will be in a less distressing form. Distressing Memory + Care Circuit = Less Distressing Memory.

This is the neurological recipe for emotional healing. In other words, you get in touch with your suffering from the past,

---

* There is very little evolutionary advantage in maintaining perfectly accurate memories of the past. Instead, your brain prioritizes improving its predictions about the future. All our memories are used to create models of how the world works so we can better predict how to keep ourselves safe and meet our needs.
** Or Play Circuit. Read about Panksepp's work in *The Archaeology of Mind*.

and connect with compassion at the same time. You embrace your pain with loving presence. If we try to process pain from the past without compassion, we end up ruminating and reinforcing our old stories. However, once we learn how to hold our suffering the way we'd hold a crying baby, real transformation becomes possible.

## PRACTICE

**Note:** There are two types of obstacles that can come up during this practice.
1. You might feel overwhelmed. That means the feeling coming up is too big for you to hold with compassion.
2. You might be unable to generate self-compassion at all.

If you notice either of those, stop the practice and skip to page 129. You can return and try again later. If you've experienced acute trauma or have a tendency to feel overwhelmed by strong emotions, do this practice with a mental health professional.

### Practice
- Choose some painful experience from your past. It's best to start with something small, not the worst thing that's ever happened to you. It can be from when you were a child or from earlier today.
- Think about that experience. Picture yourself at about the time it happened. You might picture the actual painful experience, or just get an image of yourself at about that time.

- When the image is clear, notice the sensations arising in your body. There might be tension, agitation, or anything like that. If the level of intensity is 4 to 7 out of 10, then you've chosen a good memory for this practice. If it's less than 4, think of something a little more difficult. If it's 8 or higher, choose a less painful memory.
- Once you have a memory that brings up some distress without being too intense, focus on the sensations in your body. Give yourself permission to feel those sensations without trying to change them. Let them stay or go; however they want. Practice like this for at least five minutes.
- Now get in touch with some source of compassion—a person or another living being who could love and accept you in that moment of suffering. It might be your adult self, someone you've known, a religious figure, an animal, or anything at all. Concentrate on that source of compassion until you feel something like warmth, openness, or a similar physiological response in your body. That lets us know that your Care Circuit is active.
- Now picture your source of compassion sending love and acceptance to the part of you that's suffering. Sending compassion could include saying kind words, shining some sort of energy, or just a loving expression. What's important is that it feels like love to you.
- Continue this practice for as long as it feels good.

This practice is a way to intentionally use memory reconsolidation to heal pain from the past. You activate a distressing memory, and then activate the Care Circuit in your brain at the same time. If you were able to complete this practice in a way that felt good, you can use it every day.

# IF YOU FELT OVERWHELMED—
# PRACTICE

Sometimes revisiting a painful memory is too intense. In that case, there are resource-building practices that can help us come back into the present moment and tap into a positive emotional state. If you've experienced acute trauma, dissociation, addiction, or if you just have a tendency to get overwhelmed by strong feelings, you should train yourself in these practices first. Once you've developed the ability to use them to regulate your emotions, then it's safer to revisit pain from your past. Try both of the following practices to see which feels more powerful for you. If neither feels good, continue to the next chapter.

## Sending Compassion

- Close your eyes and see if you can picture someone or something that brings up natural and uncomplicated warmth and love. It can be a baby, an animal, a baby animal, or anything at all.
- Once you have that image, let it be as clear as possible. Notice the sensations in your body. Do you feel warmth, openness, or anything like that? Allow the feelings in your body to be as strong as they want to be.
- With the image clearly in your mind, try saying these phrases, but feel free to change them or drop them if they don't help. Try saying, "May you be happy. May you be healthy. May you be safe. May you be loved." If the positive sensations in your body are growing stronger, then continue to repeat those phrases.
- Practice this for as long as it feels good.

**Receiving Compassion**
- Close your eyes and see if you can picture a person or another living being that you feel could love and accept you exactly as you are. It could be someone you've known, a religious figure, a white light, or anything at all.
- Once you have that image, let it be as clear as possible. Notice the sensations in your body. Do you feel warmth, openness, or anything like that? Allow the feelings in your body to be as strong as they want to be.
- See if you can feel their love and acceptance. Let it into your body.
- Now picture that being saying to you, "May you be happy. May you be healthy. May you be safe. May you be loved." You can change those phrases or drop them if they don't feel right. If the positive sensations in your body are growing stronger, then continue to repeat the phrases.
- Practice this for as long as it feels good.

# CHAPTER 9

# YOU'RE NOT CRAZY

The most common way people give up their power is
by thinking they don't have any.

—ALICE WALKER

spent most of my twenties in a long-distance relationship with a woman who was a terrible match for me. She was in medical school in Denver while I lived in Oakland. Back then, I wasn't just dumb and in love. I was uncommonly stupid to the point of being self-destructive. Despite my friends telling me—in no uncertain terms—that I was making a huge mistake, I clung to the relationship like a fucking barnacle.

On one hand, she was beautiful, brilliant, witty, and incredibly charming. Our phone conversations were podcast-worthy—bouncing through multiple academic subjects, classical and avant-garde art, and always hysterically funny. On the other hand, she would only give me any affection if I had just done something extraordinary. She was capable of thousand-watt expressions of love, but reserved them for moments I'd said something insightful or funny, or done something creative or special for her.

If my jokes weren't landing, or worse, if I was struggling in some way, she would completely withdraw her affection. This kept me constantly writing her songs and flying out to surprise her (despite the fact that I was working part-time on a construction crew and had almost no money). It also kept me miserable.

The particular hell vortex of our relationship would start because I was having a hard day, or because I'd just put a ton of effort into doing something to make her happy, and she was too tired from med school to give me the affection I was looking for. Either way, I wanted some love and wasn't getting it. I'd feel rejected, and in her eyes I'd become less impressive, which would cause her to withdraw further. It would get to the point that I'd literally beg her to say something nice to me, and she'd refuse to do it.

If you were a friend of mine during this era, I'm really sorry for the shit I put you through. I was a mess about this relationship, always complaining about the same things but never willing to leave. I told people that she was so much smarter and funnier than any other woman I'd met. If I left this relationship, I'd never find someone like her again. This was, of course, completely wrong, and everyone could see it but me. Sometimes I think about how much more fun I'd have had in my twenties if I'd just dated people who lived in my city. But that's revisionist history, and instead I was too busy being a dumbfuck.

## OR MAYBE I WASN'T A DUMBFUCK

I acknowledge that I definitely *seemed* like an irrational, inscrutable dumbfuck while I wasted precious years of my youth in a miserable relationship. However, a lot of people do things like this. We sabotage ourselves, act against our better judgment, or fail to do what we *completely know* would make life better. Just saying that we're being stupid doesn't help us. We need a way to make sense of these behaviors so we can hopefully do something different—or at least not feel so guilty.

There's one basic fact about the human brain that can make this type of behavior much easier to understand. It's this: our brains don't just think one thought at a time. In fact, in any given moment, there are literally millions (some researchers say billions) of relatively distinct mental processes happening in your brain. Right now, your brain is regulating your heartbeat, maintaining your sense of balance, transforming abstract shapes on paper (or a screen) into words and ideas, and comparing those ideas to your past experiences. Your brain is doing all of that at once with almost no effort from you.

When all of these processes are working together and relatively harmonious, we get to live in the pleasant fiction that we're one person who thinks one thing and feels one way. It's only when conflicts arise that we become aware of this multiplicity at all. For example, if you feel ambivalent about starting a new job—like, both excited and anxious—that can be because two different parts of you perceive your situation in two different ways.

Objectively, you're looking at an unpredictable situation, but different parts of you assess that situation differently. Imagine that one neural network in your brain is made out of the memories of all the times that change has been a good thing in your life. It would say that your present situation roughly fits in its category (we could call it *new start = life gets better*). It would see this new beginning and activate positive emotions in you.

Another neural network in your brain could be made of the memories of past failures. It would look at the same objective situation but perceive it very differently. This neural network is looking for any indications of a possible failure, and some of the elements of your new job might match its categories, too, (for example, *meeting new people = they're sometimes mean*; and *trying something new = failure*). That neural network would activate negative emotions. These two separate appraisals create two distinct emotional reactions in your brain and body. At the same time, your lived experience is "I feel mixed about it."

Whenever people seem irrational or self-destructive, recognizing this kind of multiplicity can make them easier to understand. It's not one person being irrational. Rather, it's different mental processes within them coming to conflicting conclusions about a single situation. Each process is making a rational conclusion based on its own limited perspective.

So what was going on with me when I told my friends, "I know I should leave, but I can't help feeling like she's too special to let go"? I can guarantee there was at least one neural network in me that was made out of my study of clinical psychology, meditation, and mountains of self-help books. It was appraising my relationship at the time and saying, "This is NOT healthy. You want to be in a relationship in which your partner will support you when you're suffering. That's pretty basic-level shit." This is why some people might say, "You knew better than to stay with her," but I think it'd be more accurate to say, "A part of me knew better."

At the same time, there was another neural network in my brain with a very different story. To understand that part, you'll have to know a little more about my childhood. I've mentioned that I grew up with an alcoholic single mother. She stopped drinking and started AA when I was about eight, but she continued to be pretty emotionally unavailable for most of my childhood. We've both grown a lot since then and get along much better now, but it's been a long road.

To this day, my mother isn't very comfortable around other people's pain. When someone she loves is upset it makes her even more upset, and every time I injured myself as a kid, she'd be way more shaken up than I was. One time I got hit by a car while riding my bike a few blocks from where we were living.

Neighbors told her and she ran down the street to see if I was okay. As I was lying on the concrete waiting for the ambulance, I remember trying to comfort her and help her calm down.

My mother is also very proud and would get really excited about my successes. This led to a pattern of intimacy pretty much identical to the terrible girlfriend. When I was strong and successful, my mom would shower me with compliments (which is her way of showing affection). When I was struggling, it would freak her out, so I'd get nothing.

I can say all this now, but I obviously didn't have this much perspective as a kid. Instead, the little neurons in my kid brain were trying to find some story to make sense of this pattern of intimacy. They were trying to create a model of who I really am and what I have to do to get the love I need. Those neurons came up with the story "Mom loves you when you deserve love, and the only way to deserve love is to be exceptional." When I met that girlfriend, that old neural network said, "BOOM! Perfect fit. She gives love only when you deserve it, so her love is more authentic than that of those weird people who love you all the time."

That kind of conditional love was addictive for me. I had to earn it, so it was really satisfying when I got it. It was profoundly familiar, and matched the core story I had about only deserving love when I'm exceptional. However, the flip side of only deserving love sometimes is the belief that most of the time I don't deserve it, which is an awful way to live.

## A TRANSFORMATIVE MOMENT

It wasn't easy for me to see the connection between the lack of love in my relationship and the lack of love in my childhood. I had a million rationales for why my girlfriend was actually perfect for me. It wasn't until a friend of mine who was a meditator and studying clinical psychology got completely fed up with my bitching and moaning that I finally saw it.

He told me to picture my girlfriend during a time that I wanted affection but was getting none. This wasn't hard because it happened all the time. Then he had me feel the sensations in my body as I begged her for some kindness. He kept this visualization going for a really long time, partially to help me get in touch with all the feelings there, and partially (I believe) out of sadism.

After sitting with these awful sensations in my body for several minutes, he asked me a question that I've since used with thousands of other people. He asked, "When is the first time you can remember feeling exactly like this?" In that one moment, all of my defenses collapsed. I saw this relationship was repeating the most painful aspects of my relationship with my mother, and once I saw it, I couldn't unsee it. It was over. We broke up that night. After being single for a while, I found that for the first time in my life I was attracted to women who were unconditionally supportive.

## THE LIFE AND DEATH
## OF A NEURAL NETWORK

What happened there? What was it about that experience that changed me so deeply? I know that if my friend had just told me that my girlfriend was a lot like my mom, I would've completely tuned him out. I know that because it'd happened more than once. However, he didn't just tell me. And he didn't just show me. He made sure he was talking to the *part of me* that was refusing to leave the relationship, and he showed that part.

It'll be helpful here to talk a little more about how the millions of neural networks in our brains work together (or fail to). When I was a kid, some of the little neurons in my brain came up with the story to explain why my mom would be affectionate sometimes but not others. They decided, "The only way to deserve love is to be exceptional." That story did a great job predicting when I would or wouldn't get love from my mom. Every time it made a correct prediction, my brain said, "This story must be true," so that neural network got stronger and it ended up becoming a core belief.

This brings us to a problem with how the brain is organized. Once a neural network's story passes a certain threshold of predictive accuracy, it becomes almost immune to counterevidence. We don't know why, but computational neuroscientists have some ideas.

The theory that makes the most sense to me goes like this:

When those neurons first came up with their story, they were on a type of probation. A high-level part of my brain was monitoring the story and paying attention to how well it predicted my mom's behavior. That high-level part of my brain was like the quality control supervisor who had access to a huge amount of information, including everything I consciously noticed. Once the story "you only deserve love when you're exceptional" made correct predictions about my mom like five thousand times in a row, the high-level monitor in my brain decided, "You're obviously true, so you're off probation. I'm going to focus my attention on some other stuff." From that point on, this story is basically unsupervised.

So what happens to a story when it's no longer being supervised? This is the point at which it becomes almost immune to counterevidence, and the reason comes from how our brains conserve processing power. All the individual stories in your brain are programmed to ignore everything that doesn't specifically relate to them. They're only supposed to wake up when they're needed. For example, the neural network in your brain in charge of polite manners is supposed to stay sleeping until manners are called for. It's supposed to notice when you sit down in a nice restaurant, wake up, and do its job.

Therefore, the part of me that believed "you only deserve love when you're exceptional" would sleep through any experience that didn't match its story. It would wake up around my mom or anyone else with a similar pattern of affection. However, when I started meeting more unconditionally supportive people in college, that neural network didn't compute them at all. They didn't fit the pattern, so they were irrelevant. That's how a core belief can be maintained for years in spite of overwhelming counterevidence. It wakes up when your life supports its story, and sleeps through anything that would challenge it.

Once that core belief in me was solidified, it profoundly shaped how I experienced intimacy. Unconditional support felt nice, but unfamiliar. On the other hand, people who were only kind when I was exceptional activated a part of my brain that told me "This is *real love*."

The reason my friend was able to help me let go of that story was that he knew how to wake it up. He knew that all the counterevidence in the world wasn't going to make a dent in a deeply held core belief if the neural network that held it was allowed to stay sleeping. So he had me visualize my girlfriend right in the middle of our most dysfunctional dynamic. He waited until he was positive that all the neural networks related to that dynamic were awake and activated. At that point, his little bit of counterevidence hit home powerfully and changed my life.

## HOW TO STAY HUMAN
## WHEN YOU HATE YOURSELF

Everybody has something about themselves they don't like, or wish were different. Some of us are self-critical. Some of us can't manage to do the things we know would make our lives better, or at least not consistently. Some of us can't stop ourselves from being overtly self-destructive and self-loathing.

In chapter 3, I talked about holding our suffering like we'd hold a crying baby. The problem is that sometimes our suffering doesn't look like a cute little baby. It looks like a fucking monster that's trying to tear our faces off. So how can we bring tenderness and compassion to the parts of ourselves that we hate?

My teacher Thich Nhat Hanh says "understanding is love." He believes that every part of the world, no matter how ugly, becomes entirely lovable when understood deeply enough. Loving the world doesn't stop us from working for social change. It doesn't stop us from actively opposing violence and oppression. In fact, it allows us to stay in that work for the long haul.

There's a really important difference here between love and approval. Learning how to love the self-critical voice in me *does not* mean agreeing with it. It means I can see that it's a manifestation of suffering, and it's trying in its own fucked-up way to find some relief. I see how our tragically beautiful human nature is present in it. It suffers, wants relief, but doesn't know how to find it. It's like a bird trapped in a building who seeks freedom and safety by slamming over and over into a closed window. I know that its deepest motivation is life-serving, which makes it possible to empathize. This clear understanding stimulates a special kind of tenderness—one that relates and wants to help.

## PRACTICE

If there's something about you that you find irrational or resistant to change, this practice is about developing the kind of understanding that leads to self-compassion and transformation.

- Think about something you'd like to change about yourself. Specifically, think of something you've tried to change but have been unsuccessful. Name it, and describe exactly how you'd like it to be different. If it's about a specific situation, name how you'd like to act or feel or think differently in that situation. Write it down.

- Now picture yourself in a scene that brings up the thing you want to change. Let the image be clear enough that you feel emotions arising in your body. Ideally, the intensity of emotion should be between 4 and 7 out of 10.

- Spend some time feeling the sensations in your body and allowing them to be as strong as they want to be. You're in touch with that thing you want to change, and you're open to whatever feelings arise. Stay focused on your body. Whatever feelings that arise are welcome.

- As you are in touch with these feelings in your body, try saying the following sentences to yourself and see if any of them feel true:
  » "There is a part of me that doesn't want to stop feeling like this or doing this to myself."
  » "There is a part of me that wants to hold on to this."
  » "There is a part of me that thinks I deserve this."

Notice if any of those sentences felt true. It's okay if they don't.

- Ask yourself, "When's the first time I can remember feeling *exactly like this*?" If you connect with a memory, picture yourself back there. If not, don't worry about it, and continue to the next step.
- Continue feeling those feelings in your body, and feeling in touch with this part of yourself. Try saying to yourself, "I'm ready to listen to you. You can tell me about your job, what you are trying to do and why it is so important. I'm not going to attack you." Notice whatever comes up.
- Make sure the thing you want to change is activated and you can feel it in your body. Look for how this behavior or story might have a life-serving purpose. Most likely it'll be a response to an emotional wound. Try to empathize with the part of you that believed this behavior or story was a solution to an important problem.
- Now you'll try to complete a sentence. Say the following sentence stem out loud and then finish it with whatever pops into your head. It doesn't need to make any sense. Do it at least five times. "I refuse to have compassion for myself (or love myself) because if I do . . ."
- Try to name the emotional wound that led to your story or behavior. Then try to describe how this story was an attempt to create meaning, or this behavior was an attempt to protect yourself.
- Hold the emotional pain with love and compassion. Hold it like you'd hold a crying baby.
- Dialogue with the part of you that's in charge of the problematic behavior or story. Don't make it into an enemy. Let it know you want to help, and gently share any information it doesn't have.

If we can learn how to love the ugly parts of ourselves, loving other people gets much easier. This is a practice of looking at something that seems bad, stupid, irrational, dysfunctional, or whatever. We look with the assumption that there's a part of us that has a beautiful life-serving purpose for holding on to something that seems negative. When that way of thinking becomes natural, it gets a lot easier to see the life-serving motivation in other people's dysfunction too.

# CHAPTER 10

# BECOMING FEARLESS

That one wants nothing to be different,
not forward, not backward, not in all eternity.
Not merely bear what is necessary,
still less conceal it . . . but love it.

—FRIEDRICH NIETZSCHE

n the summer of 2005, I was heading to Plum Village, the Buddhist monastery in France where Thich Nhat Hanh lives, to practice and study with him for three months. I had the summer off from graduate school, and the monks had offered me a work-exchange position, so I could stay for free. I spent my last dollar on a plane ticket and packed everything I owned into my pickup truck. The plan was to park the truck in a vehicle storage place on my way to the airport.

However, plans change. The night before my flight, I crashed on a friend's couch in Oakland. When I woke, there was a little pile of broken glass where my truck and all my earthly possessions (including my passport) had been. Everything was gone. I had no money, no place to live, and no belongings other than the clothes on my back. I had a round-trip ticket to France, but no passport. Worst of all, it seemed like my chance to study with my teacher was gone. Yet in that moment of losing everything, I smiled.

There's a story in which the Buddha was sitting on a hill with a crowd of monks enjoying the little bit of food they had begged for that day. As they ate, a farmer came running up the path. He was crying and screaming. He said to the Buddha, "Monk, have you seen my cows? When I woke up this morning they were gone. I have just a few cows and nothing else in the world. Insects destroyed my little sesame crop a few weeks ago. If I don't find my cows, I will be ruined and I will have to kill myself. Please, monk, tell me if they've passed this way."

The Buddha looked at the farmer with eyes full of compassion and said, "I'm sorry, but your cows haven't come this way. You should look in another direction." The farmer cried out and ran off. Once he was gone, the Buddha looked back at his fellow monks and gave them a big smile. He said, "How lucky you are that you have no cows to lose."

These monks had given up everything to live in the forest and beg for food. In fact, the Pali word we usually translate as "monk" is *bhikkhu*, which actually just means beggar. To me, this story is about the fearlessness that comes from letting go. There's an enormous difference between losing your cows and letting them go. Either way, you end up with no cows, but one is excruciating and the other is liberating.

Letting go of your cows doesn't mean that you don't love them, or even that you have to get rid of them. It's more of a state of mind in which you're clear that life would continue to be beautiful even if your cows were gone. Your cows can stay or go, and you'll be okay either way. In fact, letting go can help us to love more unconditionally. Once I've let go of a thing or a person, I become so much better able to appreciate them when they're present because I'm not constantly afraid of losing them.

So when I wandered outside that morning and saw my truck was gone, I actually laughed and said to myself, "Now you have no truck to lose." We called the police, and my friend stayed to fill out the report while I got a ride to the US passport agency in downtown San Francisco. Somehow they got me a replacement passport in time to make my flight. As I crossed the Atlantic, seven miles above the waves, I felt incredibly light and content.

Sadly, however, I'm not always so graceful. Just this afternoon I felt like a complete failure in my practice. As I write this, Annie is in the middle of a torturous treatment regimen. She's receiving daily radiation with continuous chemotherapy, and she's scheduled for another surgery tomorrow morning. Radiation is fucking terrible, and she's in a debilitating amount of physical pain most of the time. On top of that, she's been staying at a place near the hospital with her mom for the past week because of the intensity of her treatment schedule, while I stay home with our son. She misses us both (but especially him).

She got to come home yesterday, and when it was time for her to leave again this afternoon, it was like tearing her away. As I walked her to the car, she told me how overwhelmed she felt. This has been the most she's been away from our son since he was born, and her physical pain is getting worse. She's also sick of surgeries. We walked and I listened to her, but if I'm honest, I wasn't really there. My body was rigid, my face was made of stone, and her words flew right by me. I could see how disappointed she was by my lack of empathy, but I felt like I had nothing more to give.

After the car drove off, I sat under a tree to reflect for a few minutes while my son played. The first thing I noticed was how ashamed I felt. I'm writing this whole book about how to stay present, but I had just completely failed during a moment when I was really needed. I felt like a fraud.

Under the tree, I paid attention to the sensation of my breath and tried to come back to the present moment. I knew I was lost in stories and commentary, so I asked myself, "What is real and true right now? What do I know for sure?" I sat quietly, and something inside me gave me permission to be a fraud. It whispered, "You can be a fraud. It's okay, and I'm still here for you." As it spoke, my whole body began to relax. My mind was blank for a minute or so, and then I heard a voice in me saying, "I don't want to be present with her. It's too much. I just want to get away." And there was enough space for that voice too.

From the spaciousness, I heard, "This feeling is human and beautiful. All living beings feel averse to suffering. This aversion is part of the life in you." I wrapped my arms around myself like a hug and allowed that aversion to be as strong as it wanted to be. I whispered to myself, "You don't want to suffer, and you don't want to see others suffer. Of course you don't." In that moment I felt compassion and acceptance washing away my stress, fear, and shame. I could see myself as a living being, no different from any other—a beautiful, tiny, and inseparable part of creation. My heart continued to open, and the beauty of life in that moment left me wordless.

Luckily, it happened that I saw Annie again later that night. Plans changed and she was able to stop by to see us before her procedure. This time was different, and I was able to be there. I sat with her, held her hand, and listened to her. That aversion to her suffering still came up in me, but this time instead of feeling ashamed, I greeted it with love. A gentle voice in me said, "Of course this hurts, and you don't want to hurt. But let's stay present because we have a chance to do a lot of good." The aversion was so much lighter when I embraced it.

It turns out that sometimes your cow is a truck, and other times it's an idea. I believe the hardest type of cow to lose is an idea about who you really are. I like to think I'm somebody who can stay present when someone I love is suffering. However, I was so attached to that image of myself that it became the exact thing that was preventing me from being present. When I gave myself permission to be a fraud, I was letting go of that image of myself. Then I was free to be fully human and unafraid.

## NONATTACHMENT TO IDEAS

We all have stories we cling to that keep us from seeing things as they truly are. You might believe you're really smart, and that belief might get in the way of admitting when you don't understand something. You might believe people of a certain political ideology are irrational assholes, and that might keep you from being able to engage in meaningful dialogue with one of them. Often, the more certain we feel about a belief, the more attached we are to it. When we get too attached to an idea, we're no longer capable of learning or real communication.

There's an old story about a university professor who visits a Zen master. The professor was a genius. He had mastered every school of philosophy and was known as the best debater in the land. He came to see the Zen master because he wanted to prove that his philosophy was superior.

The Zen master invited him to sit down and offered him some tea. Then, in an adversarial tone, the professor asked, "What are the essential teachings of Zen?" At this, the Zen master began pouring the tea into the professor's cup. He filled the cup, and then continued pouring, as it overflowed onto the floor. The professor tried to keep his composure, but eventually he shouted, "The cup is full! There's no more room!" The Zen master stopped pouring and said, "It's the same with your mind. You are so full of opinions and ideas that there's no room for Zen." Shunryu Suzuki-roshi, the founder of San Francisco Zen Center, summarized the story by saying, "In the beginner's mind there are many possibilities, in the expert's mind there are few."

The value of stories like this is that they give us permission not to know everything. Not only do I not have to pretend that I have it all figured out, but there is actually virtue in admitting how little I know for sure. When I can hold my own beliefs with a degree of nonattachment, I become open to learning from life. I can let go of a belief as soon as it no longer serves me. However, the problem with stories like this is that they can make it sound sexy to say nothing and do nothing because all of our ideas are just obstacles to some sort of deeper understanding. We can end up complacent, and now is not a time in history for complacence.

## THOUGHTS ARE MODELS.
## THOUGHTS ARE TRAPS.
## THOUGHTS ARE FRIENDS.

Attachment to ideas is one of the most vicious destroyers of human connection. A real human being is the continuation of countless nonself elements, including their ancestors, teachers, and those who've harmed them. A real human being is animated by a force that seeks to avoid suffering and find wellness but often doesn't know how to do that. However, most of the time we don't interact with real human beings. We interact with our ideas and projections about them.

I have a story about what motivates my aunt to support Trump. I have a story about how my fourth-grade teacher was emotionally abusive. I have a story that my friend Gary is a misunderstood genius. If you tell me I'm wrong about any of those stories, I'll fight back. I'm emotionally invested in believing they're true, which I fully recognize is stupid.

Stories like these are mental models of human beings— dramatically simpler than the real thing. When I'm attached to my story about someone, it means I'm not open to the reality of that person. Being attached means that if my model doesn't match with reality, I choose to keep the model. Fuck reality.

Nonattachment means being more interested in reality than in models. It starts with recognizing that all of my ideas are just models of the world; they aren't the world itself. An idea can never match reality perfectly, just like a map can never match the terrain perfectly. Even if a map has no serious errors, it'll always be a simplification. Trying to fully comprehend the reality of any situation is like the Borges story about the cartographers who want to create a perfect map of their empire. They end up with a map that's the same size as the empire. It's ridiculous.

When we forget that our ideas are just models of the world, they become traps. My aunt is not incapable of reason, but my mental model of her is. My fourth-grade teacher is not the embodiment of evil, but my mental model of her is. My friend Gary is not infallible, but my mental model of him is. Real connection and real learning are only possible when I'm open to letting go and updating my models of people and the world.

Most of us believe everything we think, which is insane. Everyone knows we're capable of misperception and misunderstanding, and we can look back on all the times we were wrong. We were sure that person at the party hated us, or we were positive the sound in the backyard was a bear, but it just wasn't true. However, somehow that doesn't stop us from completely believing whatever we happen to think next. It's like we can admit a past thought was inaccurate, but whatever we're thinking in the present just seems so real.

The way of relating to our thoughts that I've found most helpful is to imagine that they're friends who constantly offer unsolicited opinions and advice. If you have a friend who really loves you, and can't stop giving you advice, how would you relate to what she says? You shouldn't immediately reject it or ignore her, because she cares about you, and she can't *always* be wrong. Yet you obviously shouldn't believe her words without question. Ideally, you'd take note of what she says, appreciate her for caring, and then inquire for yourself before you decide if something is worth believing.

The more we learn about how the mind works, the more possible it becomes not to get caught in our stories. Many computational neuroscientists are kind of obsessed with something called the *Bayesian brain hypothesis*. Basically, it means that our models of the world are primarily about trying to predict what'll happen in the future. Some models, such as phrenology, are terrible at predicting. The shape of your neighbor's skull will tell you nothing about how likely he is to rob you. Other models, such as Newtonian physics, are pretty accurate. If I hit a cue ball with a certain force at a certain angle, I can predict with a lot of accuracy where it will end up.

According to the Bayesian brain hypothesis, we can develop increasing certainty about our beliefs based on every time they succeed at predicting something. However, certainty can never reach 100 percent because they're just models based on incomplete information.

If we can train ourselves to see our present worldview as an approximation of reality that can always be updated with new experience, we develop the kind of cognitive flexibility that allows us to learn, grow, and connect. We avoid the trap of complete relativism, because our beliefs are grounded in our experience of the world. We also avoid the trap of complete certainty, because we know that our beliefs are just models.

## PRACTICE

- Choose a belief you hold that someone else would argue against.
- Think about it, and allow yourself to feel completely certain that you're right and they're wrong.
- As you hold that belief in your mind, pay attention to the sensations in your body.
- Give yourself permission to feel those sensations, and allow them to be as strong as they want to be.
- Say to yourself, "It's all right for me to feel certain about my belief. I don't need to fight against that." Continue feeling the sensations in your body.
- Direct love and acceptance toward whatever distress you feel.
- Wait until your body begins to feel a little calmer, and try saying to yourself, "My belief is a model of the world based on my experience, but it is not the world itself." Notice the sensations that arise in your body, and feel them. Welcome whatever comes up in you and spend a few minutes with it.
- When your body feels somewhat calm, picture your opponent arguing against you. Try saying to yourself, "This person's belief is their model of the world based on their experience. I know their deepest motivation is to reduce suffering."
- Finally, ask yourself, "If I could add my experience to theirs, what model would make sense of both?"

## ACTING WITH CONVICTION
## BUT WITHOUT CERTAINTY

As you reflect on all of this, you might question how nonattachment to ideas would change your ability to act. For example, how am I supposed to create change in the world if I always doubt my beliefs? How can I stay open and nonattached to ideas without getting complacent? How can I take a stand against something I know is wrong without falling into the traps of certainty, like toxic righteousness and dehumanizing my opponents?

Gandhi wrote a lot about his struggles with these questions. He believed the key was to recognize that his current perspective would never be changeless, absolute truth. Yet it would always have some kernel of truth in it. He would advocate passionately for what he believed to be true while trying to remain open to the kernels of truth he believed must exist in the perspectives of his opponents.

That might sound great, but it's easier said than done. In reality, people who are open to learning from different perspectives are often pretty complacent. They might be compassionate with the people in their lives, but they're much less likely to be actively engaged in trying to oppose violence and oppression. On the other hand, people who are on the front lines of working for social change are often really attached to their ideas and not particularly open to learning. However, it doesn't have to be this way. Some of the most effective social movements in history have held nonattachment to views as a primary value. We can do that again, and if we do, I believe we'll find our activism to be much more impactful.

## BECOMING FEARLESS

Nonattachment to ideas can be a gateway to radical fearlessness, because all of our fear and anger (and sometimes even our grief) begin when our mind labels some situation as *unacceptable*. It could be something that's already happening or that might happen. The label of *unacceptable* triggers the threat-response system in your brain and body. It creates negative emotions that mobilize you to change or prevent the threat. In that psychological state, you have very little access to deliberate thought. Instead, you'll mostly react on autopilot.

On the other hand, fearlessness becomes possible when we face a threat and examine it until our mind no longer views it as unacceptable. Once it becomes acceptable, it's no longer a threat, and the fear is gone. You might still choose to change or prevent the situation—you even might use all your power to try—but you'll do it with freedom and nonattachment. Change becomes a preference instead of an absolute requirement, which creates a tremendous amount of lightness, openness, and humanity.

This is how it works: There's some situation in your life, or something you're worried might happen, that's bothering you. It might be completely freaking you out, or just distracting you. Either way, you recognize that there's some situation that your mind has deemed unacceptable. Again, it might be something that's already happened, or it might just be something that *could* happen. For the purpose of this practice, we'll treat them the same.

Direct your attention to the objective situation. Try to separate the observable reality from your stories about it. For example, the observable reality is your partner crying and saying, "I can't believe you did that." The story might be that this reaction means you're a terrible person.

As you bring your full presence to this scene, embrace the sensations that arise in your body. Hold them like you'd hold a crying baby—with warmth, tenderness, and loving attention. You're facing some aspect of reality, and allowing your body to have a negative response. Stress hormones like cortisol and adrenaline might be racing through your bloodstream as you offer yourself complete love and acceptance. As you embrace your experience with compassion, this activates your brain's Care Circuit, which begins to regulate your emotions. The whole time, you continue to focus on the scene that you had labeled *unacceptable*.

Your mind might jump from this scene to others, like if this happens, it could lead to that, which would be even worse. For the purpose of this practice, don't fight it. In fact, real fear-lessness comes from being open to the absolutely worst-case scenario your mind can create. Without believing this scenario definitely will happen, you allow the possibility that it *could happen.* Face your worst-case scenario while embracing your fear with love.

Eventually something will open. Your brain will recognize that even the worst case it can imagine might not be as bad as it seemed. It will perceive that even if the worst thing comes to pass, love will still be possible. Now, as you face that situation, your physiological response is different. The situation is the same, but it no longer inspires such fear or anger. Grounded in self-compassion, you can choose to act or not act with freedom and space. That's the state I call fearlessness.

# CHAPTER 11

# COMMUNITY AS REFUGE, COMMUNITY AS WEAPON

Human beings *will* be happier—
not when they cure cancer or get to Mars . . .
but when they find ways to inhabit
primitive communities.

—KURT VONNEGUT

L et's look at three quotes about community, and then think about what they mean together. In the Upaddha Sutta, the Buddha is having a conversation with his attendant Ananda. Ananda says that after all his years of meditation practice he's come to believe that having good spiritual friends is half of the path, and he asks the Buddha if he agrees. The Buddha says:

> *Don't say that, Ananda. Having good spiritual*
> *friends is not half of the path. It is actually the*
> *entirety of the path. When someone has good spiritual*
> *friends, you can expect they will develop and pursue*
> *the holy life.*

So the Buddha says spiritual friendship is everything when it comes to spiritual development. In fact, the community of practitioners, often called *Sangha*, is considered one of the

Three Jewels of Buddhism, on equal footing with the Buddha and his teachings.

Our second quote is attributed to the feminist and anthropologist Margaret Mead. While no one is certain she ever said it, it's become one of the most often quoted statements among activists. The quote is:

*Never doubt that a small group of thoughtful,*
*committed people can change the world.*
*Indeed, it is the only thing that ever has.*

I can confirm that every social movement of which I've been a part has been held together by closely knit personal relationships. So good spiritual friends are the only way to grow spiritually, and good activist friends might be the only way to create change.

Now, our third quote comes from Vivek Murthy, former US surgeon general. In 2018, he wrote:

*Loneliness is a growing health epidemic. We live in the*
*most technologically connected age in the history of*
*civilization, yet rates of loneliness have doubled since*
*the 1980s.*

In other words, our society is largely missing the single factor that makes spiritual growth and social change possible: community.

According to Murthy, Americans report being lonelier and more isolated than they have at any time in history, with nearly half of all adults saying they don't have meaningful in-person social interactions daily. Although most of us assume that elderly people are the most isolated, in reality Gen Z (by some definitions, those born after 1997) reports a higher level of loneliness than any other generation. Moreover, social isolation is not only spiritually and politically disabling, research has shown that loneliness is as bad for your health as smoking a pack of cigarettes a day. It is literally killing us.

So what are we supposed to do? Should we all throw away our cell phones and escape into the mountains, like in the movie *Captain Fantastic*? Should we all join communes? It seems clear that our society's devastating lack of community isn't going to be solved by a new social media platform, but it's not clear what actually could help.

I wish I had a prepackaged solution for this problem, but I don't. However, it seems to me that any solution has to begin with the recognition of the central importance of community in our lives, and the willingness to prioritize it over other things. It will have to include making individual choices, as well as collective action to resist the larger socioeconomic trends that directly and indirectly oppose community and sociality.

In this chapter, therefore, I'll share some of my story of attempting to prioritize community in my life, and I'll offer a few suggestions and some space for you to reflect.

## CHOOSING COMMUNITY

In the spring of 2011, Annie and I quit our jobs, packed our shit, and left California to move to New Hampshire. You might be thinking, "Why would anyone do that?" which also happened to be what a lot of our friends were thinking.

Here's why: A few years earlier, I had been on meditation retreat at Plum Village and heard that two of my favorite monastics, Fern and Michael, had left the monastery and were going to get married. I got in touch with them, and they explained that they were planning to start a new project unlike anything I'd heard of. It would basically be a monastery for laypeople—a place where people who don't want to take monastic vows (such as celibacy or not owning anything) could live together in community and host meditation retreats. It would be a place to live simply, close to nature, and prioritize mindfulness and togetherness.

Annie and I spent a few years flirting with the idea. We'd visit Fern and Michael in New England and talk with them about their vision for the community. At the same time, we were really enjoying life in the Bay Area. We loved the progressive culture, the arts, the weather, and Annie grew up in San Francisco, so it's her hometown. We also had stable jobs. I was the director of a program in Oakland for children with severe emotional disturbances, and Annie was the director of a farm-based environmental education center in nearby Marin County.

On the other hand, life in California has downsides. Working for nonprofits, we'd always struggle to pay rent in the Bay Area. We also knew we wanted to start a family, and we saw that our friends with kids had become incredibly busy, stressed, and even more strapped for cash.

We struggled for a long time about what to do. Eventually, for us, the Bay Area came to symbolize stable money, urban culture, and the kind of career/family path we saw everyone else taking. On the other hand, joining Fern and Michael was like jumping into the unknown. We didn't have a plan for making money, but we wouldn't need nearly as much. We hoped there would be a strong community, but it would be just our two families to start.

After sitting on the fence for three years, we finally made the jump. In the meantime, Fern and Michael had fund-raised enough money to buy 240 acres of forest near Keene, New Hampshire, which was cheap because it'd been used as a dump by locals for thirty years. They cleaned it up, built a house and small meditation hall out of straw bales and clay. They'd told us we could have a spot to build a house for ourselves if we'd come and help them start the project. So we did it. It felt like letting go of everything stable and predictable to make space for community and simplicity.

When we arrived, I made a little money writing and working with therapy clients over the phone, but mostly we focused on building a house and starting the retreat center/cohousing community. We called it MorningSun Mindfulness Center, and we still live there. Since we built the house ourselves, it didn't cost much, and we've been perfectly comfortable living well below the federal poverty line.

## COMMUNITY IS REFUGE
## (FROM EVERYTHING BUT YOURSELF)

For me, living at MorningSun has been a huge blessing. I don't need much money, so I'm never that busy. There are almost always people around who are available to talk or do something with. Since Annie's diagnosis, we've had an incredible amount of support. Moreover, I can't imagine having better conditions to support my mindfulness practice. However, living in community doesn't fix everything.

You've probably heard the saying "Wherever you go, there you are." Living in community hasn't stopped me from feeling lonely, frustrated, and stressed out, because it's still life, and those are mental states that will arise in any environment, no matter how supportive. I think the most we hope for from a living situation is one in which we have enough space and support that we can pay attention to our suffering and care for it.

## COMMUNES AREN'T FOR EVERYONE

Living at MorningSun might sound idealistic, but it's obviously not a solution for everyone. In fact, as much as Annie loves our community, she also really misses her roots in California, so it's not even clear how long we'll stay.

The fact is that we're going to need a lot of different solutions to the problem of social isolation if our society is going to recover any sense of community. Some people will be willing to make major lifestyle-disrupting changes to find simplicity and connection. However, most people are interested in growing community where they are.

In that case, it seems there are a few broad questions to explore.

1. If you're overcommitted, can you create more space in your life for connection?
2. Are there things you do alone (or with your nuclear family) that could potentially be done in community?
3. Do you have emotional blocks to connection and intimacy?

I don't have a lot to say about the first two questions, other than to recommend that you take some time and space to reflect on them and be creative. However, I do have something to say about the third.

If you recognize there might be a part of you that's holding you back from greater connection and intimacy, the first thing to do is assess whether the people in your life are capable of the kind of intimacy you want. Intimacy always requires vulnerability. In fact, in some ways they're the same thing. We feel close to someone to the extent that we can be vulnerable with them, which means exposing ourselves to emotional risk.

Can you think of anyone in your life who would respond positively if you took the risk of sharing more of yourself? If you can't, you might need to consider making new friends (meditation groups can be places to start). However, if you can think of someone, then your practice is going to be about tolerating the risk of emotional exposure.

If that's the case, try this practice:

## PRACTICE

- Picture the other person and imagine telling them something true and vulnerable about yourself. You can start small. For example, say something that makes you feel insecure or something about yourself you wish were different.
- Pay attention to the sensations that arise in your body as you say this. Allow those sensations to be as strong as they want to be. Let them stay or change however they want. Spend at least a few minutes just feeling and accepting. You are taking this risk, and some unpleasant sensations might come up in your body. Don't fight them. Let yourself feel them and remember how universal these feelings are.
- Stay with the image of sharing something vulnerable with the person you chose, and stay connected with the sensations in your body. Now send compassion to yourself. You might try saying kind words to the part of you

that's suffering, imagine directing an energy of love toward yourself, or picture someone whom you feel could love and accept you right in that moment. The important part is getting in touch with the insecurity of being vulnerable and having the experience of being loved *at the same time.*

Continue with this practice until you can imagine sharing something vulnerable while feeling somewhat comfortable. At that point, contact your chosen person and try this in real life.

## COMMUNITY AS WEAPON

In 1966, the Vietnam War was escalating, and Thich Nhat Hanh was working tirelessly with the School of Youth for Social Service to help victims and rebuild villages. He and the people working closest with him were also constantly at the edge of despair. It had been three years since his close friend Thích Quảng Đức set himself on fire to protest the war. They were doing everything in their power to try to end the devastation, but things were only getting worse.

On the full-moon day in February of that year, Thich Nhat Hanh and five of his closest friends held a ceremony in Saigon to formally establish the Order of Interbeing (Tiếp Hiện). It was three women and three men, some monastics and some laypeople, who took vows to support each other's mindfulness practice and work together for social change. They would hold at least one day a week for meditation, and they would support each other in every possible way.

This is a perfect example of how communities can serve the dual functions of emotional refuge and instrument of political action. Just like meditation practice, our communities can embrace us when we're suffering, and they can strengthen us in our work for a better world. If they're only a refuge, they'll become navel-gazing and escapist. If they're only focused on action, they'll be emotionally cold and feed our toxic righteousness. A healthy community can move back and forth between these functions depending on what we need.

Thich Nhat Hanh would also warn his students against trying to practice mindfulness without the support of a community. He said it's like a raindrop landing on the top of a mountain and hoping to make it all the way to the ocean by itself. There's no way. However, if it can go as part of a river, reaching its destination becomes possible. If we can find people who share our aspirations, our collective energy becomes a river carrying us in the direction we want to go.

CHAPTER 12

# YOUR TEN THOUSAND HOURS

[Meditation] seems to me the most
luxurious and sumptuous response to the
emptiness of my own existence.

—LEONARD COHEN

f you've read this far, hopefully some of the ideas and practices in this book have resonated with you. This final chapter is about how to take whatever ideas you've liked and integrate them as deeply as possible into *who you are*. It's about moving from thought into action, and using practice to create new habits.

The first part of this chapter is about how to practice in a way that makes you feel more alive. The second part focuses on the nuts and bolts of creating a meditation practice that fits you.

## DON'T BE A MINDFULNESS ZOMBIE

If you spend much time around retreat centers or meditation groups, it's easy to get the impression that the main effect of mindfulness practice is to make people sheepish and repressed. I call these people *mindfulness zombies*. They walk slowly, speak gently, and bow deeply, but talking with them is like talking with someone in a cult. They don't seem to have any of their own thoughts or feelings. Instead, they parrot back whatever dharma words they've been reading about that week. In some places, they run so deep it can seem like the only way to fit in as a new meditator is to act like they do. Please don't.

The whole point of practicing mindfulness, compassion, gratitude, and all of this is to be more fully alive. It's about strengthening your capacity to be fully human, which means feeling at home and comfortable with the entire spectrum of human experience. It's the opposite of trying to restrict yourself to a narrow band of acceptable expression.

In every moment of your practice, stay in touch with what's alive in you. If you're just going through the motions, you won't get nearly as much benefit. There are two factors that I've found can be extremely helpful here. They're motivation and confidence. In Buddhist psychology, motivation (Pali: *viriya*) comes from knowing that something is beneficial. You strengthen this capacity by reflecting on the benefits of cultivating compassion, fearlessness, or whatever quality you want to practice, as well as the dangers of not doing so.

In my life, I find it incredibly helpful to connect with my motivation before engaging in any type of meditation practice. I ask, "Why am I doing this?" If the answer is, "This practice is to develop more concentration," then I'll ask myself why that matters. Why is it worth my time? I don't always need to answer these questions. Just asking them helps keep me in touch with what's alive in me, and keeps me from going through the motions.

For me, when meditation becomes rote, it gets lifeless and offers almost no benefit. In Plum Village, there's a practice of bowing to the altar at the end of any event in the meditation hall. If I bow because everyone else is bowing, it's worse than a waste of time. It becomes an obstacle that keeps me from really being in touch with life. Instead I'll ask myself, "Why should I bow?" which reminds me to use that moment to acknowledge my gratitude for the tradition I'm learning. In that way, the moment comes to life.

I want to be a more loving, accepting, and fearless person. I want to be a source of compassion and joy in the lives of the people I love. I can't think of anything I want more than that, so it's what motivates me to practice.

In Buddhist psychology, confidence (Pali: *saddha*) comes from knowing something is possible, and that it's possible for you. Maybe I'm really clear about my aspiration, like I know I want to have a more open heart or to confront injustice with fearlessness. However, if I doubt whether it's possible for me, then I won't practice with nearly as much energy. When you know that developing your capacity to stay human is beneficial and possible, you'll be able to sustain your practice.

## YOU DON'T HAVE TO GIVE UP ANYTHING, BUT YOU HAVE TO BE WILLING TO

In every moment of modern life, your phone, your job, your favorite TV show, and every other fucking thing will constantly chirp at you, "Pay attention to me. I'm what matters." There are hundreds of thousands of intelligent and well-paid professionals who are working tirelessly to develop new ways to grab your attention. If you allow your precious attention to go wherever it's called, you'll end up a shell of a human being. Instead, we have to know what matters and make deliberate choices.

The next precondition for creating real change in your life is making space to prioritize your practice. Making space doesn't always mean you have to sacrifice other things that are important to you, but sometimes it does. In the long term, developing your capacity to stay human will definitely help your career, family, friendships, and just about everything else. However, there'll be times when you'll have to choose where to focus your limited time and energy.

If you plan to devote a full day to practice, that means you won't be able to be other places. If you prioritize developing mindfulness and compassion, there will be times when you'll be forced to choose between your practice and something else that wants your immediate attention. In my experience, the feeling of abundance doesn't come from trying to "have it all," if having it all means adding more and more to your life without ever being willing to put something down. For me, abundance comes from simplifying and being happy with less.

---

**PRACTICE**

- Make a list of everything in your life that is more important to you than cultivating your capacity to stay human.
- Make a list of everything that is less important.
- Reflect on how much time you allocate to things that are less important and consider ways to devote more energy to the things that matter most.

---

## MAKING YOUR PRACTICE DELIBERATE

Malcolm Gladwell's bestselling book *Outliers* popularized the concepts of *deliberate practice* and the *ten-thousand-hour rule*, both of which come from the pioneering work of psychologist Anders Ericsson. Ericsson studies how people improve at anything, from sports to music to memory. His research led him to believe that nearly every type of expert practices their craft in a similar way, which he calls deliberate practice. According to Gladwell, ten thousand hours of deliberate practice is a good rough estimate for what it takes to develop expertise in any field.

I play guitar, and I wish I were better at it. The problem is that 98 percent of the time I've spent playing guitar over the course of my life has been playing songs that aren't particularly challenging for me. Then, if I make a mistake, I just keep going.

Deliberate practice, on the other hand, is something different. It means choosing a specific skill I want to improve and focusing on it. It means paying attention to my mistakes and correcting them immediately, ideally with the support of a teacher. Finally, it means gradually increasing the level of difficulty so that I'm always challenged but never overwhelmed. Every hour spent doing that would count as an hour of deliberate practice. On the other hand, every hour I spend around a campfire strumming the same three chords would not.

I believe the three conditions of deliberate practice also apply to developing our capacity to stay human.

1. We choose a specific skill we hope to develop (such as gratitude, self-compassion, or fearlessness), and we work on it. It's even possible to bring this type of intentionality to developing effortlessness and tranquility. We just spend twenty minutes letting go of the desire to accomplish anything.

2. We utilize feedback immediately. If our practice feels lifeless, we come back to the here and now and ask if there might be a more beneficial way to relate to the present moment. We might switch from observing our feelings to embracing them, or from focusing on suffering to focusing on joy. Ideally, we'd have a teacher to help, but the important part is that we notice when practice feels unhelpful and respond as best we can.

3. We increase the level of difficulty. For example, once you're able to find some serenity alone on your cushion, you might start visualizing a challenging person in your life and sending them compassion.

Start by choosing one or more specific qualities you'd like to grow in yourself. When you do this, DO NOT use it as an opportunity for self-criticism—or at least try not to. If you find that it's impossible for you to think about qualities you'd like to develop without being mean to yourself, then I recommend self-compassion as the first skill to focus on.

Once you've settled on a few specific qualities, the next step is to learn about them. You want to develop a basic level of intellectual understanding. What is gratitude, and what are a few common ways to develop it? How is self-compassion different from self-esteem or self-pity?

When you have an intellectual grasp of the quality you want to develop, start experimenting with different ways to put it into practice. Lots of teachers will offer wildly varying advice. Try things out and see what feels helpful for you. Finally, use whatever practices you've found helpful to train yourself.

## THE BEST REASON TO MEDITATE

During a retreat at Plum Village, Thich Nhat Hanh asked all of his students why the Buddha continued to meditate after his enlightenment. No one was brave enough to answer, so he kept asking. Why did the Buddha continue to meditate after his enlightenment? He let us contemplate the question for a little while, and eventually said that he thought he knew the answer. He said, "I believe he continued to meditate because he liked to."

He went on to emphasize that if you can't find a way to practice that you enjoy, you'll never persevere. He said that we must all find ways to practice that we like. Even when we're embracing our suffering, there should be some sweetness and relief that we feel. Finally, he repeated that the best reason to meditate is because you like to. If your reason to practice is that you believe something about you is unacceptable, then that belief will color your practice and undermine your efforts. Instead, consider thinking like this: "What could be a better use of a human life than growing my compassion?" Then find ways to do so that bring you joy.

## FOUR FORMS OF PRACTICE

There are so many different ways to practice mindfulness that it can be overwhelming to decide what to prioritize in your own life. I'll break it down into four major categories as a way to help you reflect on what might be the best fit for you. I recommend experimenting with different forms until you find at least one that you like from each category.

## Retreats

There are so many retreat centers and monasteries in the United States and around the world that offer a huge range of programs. This kind of intensive immersion experience can be one of the best ways to deepen your meditation practice. It can also be an excellent first step for someone who is just starting to practice meditation. Sometimes sitting for twenty minutes on your own can be difficult for beginners because it's hard to settle into a practice. However, after a few days on retreat, even a complete beginner will often have a deep-enough experience that it can become the foundation for their daily practice at home.

When deciding what kind of retreat to try, there are a lot of things to consider. Obviously, location and finances are important. There are more retreat centers in the Northeast and on the West Coast compared to many other areas of the country, so people who live in other areas might decide they want to travel to find a place that feels right. There is also a huge range of costs for retreats, from Goenka-style Vipassana retreats that are completely free of charge (you are asked to make a voluntary donation only after you've completed a course) to spa-like centers that charge up to $1,000 a day or more.

Then you might consider whether you want to go to a center that is Christian, Buddhist, secular, or of another tradition. Would you prefer a center that is run by a staff of laypeople or monastics? Do you want a solo retreat experience where you are alone in a cabin all day (many retreat centers offer this option), or would you prefer participating in a structured retreat schedule with others? Would you like a retreat that is totally silent (the Goenka-style retreats mentioned above involve ten days in total silence in a group), or would you prefer some periods of silence as well as time to connect with others?

If there are teachers you admire, there is nothing like practicing alongside them. I recommend familiarizing yourself with teachers such as the Dalai Lama, Pema Chödrön, Jack Kornfield, Tara Brach, Sharon Salzberg, and Ajahn Amaro. If you can attend a retreat with a master teacher, it's really worth it.

Personally, I like Plum Village retreats because the monks and nuns who lead them also live in their monasteries year-round and have dedicated their entire lives to developing mindfulness and compassion. They have taken vows of poverty and chastity to devote all of their energy to practice. These retreats are like temporarily joining a living community of people who have integrated mindfulness into every aspect of their lives.

Also, Plum Village–style retreats are not merely focused on silent sitting meditation. Instead, you are encouraged to treat every moment of the day as a form of meditation. This includes formal practices of sitting and chanting, as well as walking, listening to teachings, small-group discussion, and eating. For me, the focus on bringing mindfulness to many different kinds of activities helps me to more fully integrate the practice into my daily life. However, it also requires significant self-discipline. With less formal structure than some other retreats, you must rely on your own diligence to treat every moment as a meditation. It's different from the highly structured Goenka-style retreats or a *sesshin* at a Soto Zen center, in which you might practice silent sitting for ten hours a day.

There are plenty of wonderful retreat centers in every part of the United States and around the world. I recommend experimenting with different kinds of retreats until you find one that you like, and then doing your best to spend at least a few days on retreat every year. When I joined the Order of Inter-being, I made a commitment to spend at least sixty days on retreat each year. That equates to one full day of practice each week and two five-day retreats a year. Whenever possible, I try to spend long periods of time studying at Plum Village.

## Moment-to-Moment Practice

It's possible to learn how to sit, walk, and breathe in ways that make happiness and peace available at any moment of life. When Thich Nhat Hanh was first ordained as a Buddhist monk, in 1942 in Vietnam, he was given a small book of poems. He was told to learn them all by heart so he could recite them throughout the day. There was a poem for waking up, one for putting on his robes, one for washing his face, and so on. This was his introduction to Buddhist monastic training. The poems were reminders to bring mindfulness and compassion to every action and every moment of life. He has adapted these poems for contemporary use in his book *Present Moment Wonderful Moment*. This is the poem for waking up:

> *Waking up this morning, I smile.*
> *Twenty-four brand-new hours are before me.*
> *I vow to live fully in each moment*
> *and to look at all beings with eyes of compassion.*

Imagine approaching every moment of life in this way. You wake up filled with gratitude and wonder at the miracle of being alive. As you sit up in bed, you are deeply aware of all the sensations in your body. You enjoy the feeling of the soft sheets and blankets, and you notice the pleasant temperature on your skin. You pause and take ten or twelve conscious breaths, completely unhurried and smiling broadly that you have clean air and functioning lungs. As you shower, you fully enjoy the experience of showering. As you eat breakfast, you bring your complete concentrated presence to every bite of food and savor the taste and texture. You feel overwhelmed with gratitude for having enough food to eat. Each action and each moment of life becomes a miracle.

This practice is also possible when life is harder. As you drive to work in heavy traffic, you can enjoy your breathing and the feeling of relaxation in your body. You might also feel grateful for the teachers and practices that help you to be happy at that moment. When you look at the clock and see that you are already ten minutes late, you could think, "I'm moving as quickly as I can, and I will arrive whenever I arrive." You don't feel rushed at all. In fact, you might begin to say to yourself, "I am arriving fully in every moment, exactly where I am." When you do arrive at work, you are refreshed and full of joy.

If that all sounds a little farfetched, then choose at least one daily activity to perform mindfully. It could be eating a meal in silence or going for a mindful walk. There are a lot of different ways to practice walking meditation, but the one that Thich Nhat Hanh teaches most often is to practice arriving in the present moment with each step. Instead of walking to arrive at some destination, you walk only to enjoy walking.

## The Support of a Community

If you try to practice alone, you rely on your own willpower to avoid getting carried away by negative habits. However, a group of like-minded people can provide a kind of collective momentum that helps you live in harmony with your values. If you sit down to meditate by yourself, you might get bored or distracted and get up after five minutes. On the other hand, you might find that sitting for twenty minutes or more is easy in a group.

## Formal Daily Practice

Formal daily practice is the time you set aside each morning or evening for explicitly cultivating whatever qualities you want to develop in yourself. Formal practices can include sitting meditation, walking meditation, prayer, chanting, studying spiritual or inspirational texts, tai chi, yoga, and listening to the sound of a bell. When you study teachings, read slowly. Reflect on what you read and seek to apply the teachings to your life, rather than just trying to accumulate knowledge.

Experiment with different types of practices to discover what works best for you. Thich Nhat Hanh has a book called *Chanting from the Heart: Buddhist Ceremonies and Daily Practices*, which describes lots of different kinds of formal practice. There are so many varieties of meditation that I believe there's something out there for everyone. If you haven't yet found one that you enjoy, keep looking. You will.

## BLUEPRINTS FOR PRACTICE

In my experience, people starting a meditation practice usually fall into three categories. I'll describe each category, and offer some recommendations for each.

### Baby Steps

If you like to start things slowly and inch your way in, here are a couple of options I'd recommend.

**Option 1.** Spend five minutes a day with one of the practices from this book, or just rereading and reflecting. Most people find the most convenient time for short periods of meditation is first thing when you wake up or just before going to sleep. Use a calendar or journal to keep track of how often you're able to do it. After a week, increase your practice time to ten minutes. Once you get consistent with ten minutes a day, increase to twenty. Then, when you're consistent with twenty minutes a day, begin looking for a meditation group or a brief retreat experience.*

**Option 2.** Download a meditation app on your phone.* Increase your practice time slowly over the course of a month. After you've become consistent with twenty minutes a day, begin looking for a meditation group or a brief retreat experience.

## Joiner

If you believe you'll have an easier time practicing with the support of a community, start by looking for a meditation group or a brief retreat experience.* Let that community be the anchor of your practice. Then ease into practicing on your own between group sessions.

## I Was Born for This

Some people learn about these practices, and it's love at first sight. That's how it was for me, and my only question was how to go as deep as possible. If that's how you're feeling, here's a blueprint for you.

---

* Recommendations at www.timdesmond.net.

- Sixty days of retreat per year. These might be done during long retreats, or by setting aside one day per week. You could be with a group, or just home alone. The important part is that you dedicate the entire day to practice, from the time you wake up until the time you go to sleep.
- Twenty minutes of sitting or walking meditation in the morning, and twenty minutes in the evening every day.
- Find a meditation group you like, and be an active member.
- Pay attention to the sensations around your heart as much as you can throughout your day. When you notice any constriction or heaviness, stop what you're doing and send yourself compassion. Practice like that until your heart feels light again.
- At least once a day, stop and ask yourself what would bring you the most joy at that moment. Just listen to the answer that arises, without evaluating. Then ask yourself if there's anything that would bring even more joy than your first answer. Continue repeating that practice until you arrive at some clarity, and then do whatever would bring you the most joy. This is a way to cultivate generosity toward yourself.

## A GUIDE TO SITTING MEDITATION

Sit in a comfortable position with your eyes open or closed. You might want to sit in a chair or on a cushion on the floor. Many people find that sitting with a straight spine helps them to feel more alert.

1. Begin by bringing your attention to the sensation of your breathing. Try to follow the physical sensations of your breath coming in and going out from the beginning until the end of each breath. Take several breaths in this way as you bring your mind back in touch with your body in the present moment. Allow yourself to enjoy the sensation of your breath and recognize that it can be a pleasant sensation.

2. After a period of focusing on your breathing, begin to direct compassion toward yourself in the present moment. Scan your body and mind for any discomfort. If there is any physical tension or emotional distress, direct compassion right at its source. Continue sending compassion to yourself, and specifically to your suffering, until you can no longer find any distress in your mind or body.

3. Finally, spend a few minutes just savoring this deep experience of wellness.

## A USER'S GUIDE TO CHAOS AND HORROR

Just a few years ago, I couldn't have written this book. When Annie and I first arrived at MorningSun Mindfulness Center, there were so many positive conditions in my life that everything I did felt effortless. I could practice meditation several hours a day, and I was surrounded by an abundance of community. Even in the middle of fifteen-hour days organizing at

Occupy Wall Street, I felt light and joyful most of the time. But that was then.

As Annie's health continues to deteriorate and our son is about to turn five, my practice today is less about how to walk on water, and more about how not to drown. The amounts of chaos and pain in my family have forced me to deepen my practice, and for that I'm thankful. I know I'm not the only one who is in danger of being overwhelmed by suffering—by personal tragedy as well as by the violence and oppression in the world. I offer you this book in the hope that my experience will benefit you in some way.

At this moment, may we sit in the middle of the storm, fully present. May we bring our complete attention to the here and now, although it might be full of uncertainty and pain. May we allow the soft animal of the body to react however it will, not asking it to be anything different than it is. May we gaze at the body and the feelings with total love and acceptance, appreciating the beauty of life in all its forms.

May we all be happy. May we all be healthy. May we all be safe. May we all be loved.

# AFTERWORD

On December 18, 2018, Annie passed away. She spent her last weeks surrounded by friends and family, saying goodbye with a radiant smile.

Through this whole experience, I'm left feeling tremendous gratitude for all the teachers who've taught me how to hold my pain and loss with compassion. Thanks to them, I can see that Annie isn't really gone. Her imprint on the world is her continuation—all the people whose lives she changed.

If she could, I believe Annie would ask us to remember her by loving fearlessly and doing everything we can to support people who are suffering. That's exactly what I plan to do.

# ACKNOWLEDGMENTS

Anything I understand about anything, I owe to Thich Nhat Hanh, the monks and nuns of Plum Village, and the other spiritual teachers I've been fortunate enough to meet in my life. I can't express the depth of my gratitude to them.

This book would not be possible without the support of everyone at MorningSun Mindfulness Center, as well as the community of activists and organizers I've been fortunate enough to work with in the ongoing movement for peace, justice, and ecological regeneration. Without you, all my hope and idealism would have died long ago.

Thank you to Stephanie Tade and Sydney Rogers for believing in me and in this project.

Most important, thank you to past generations and our beloved dead. We are the waves, and you are the water.

# ABOUT THE AUTHOR

**TIMOTHY AMBROSE DESMOND** is a Distinguished Faculty Scholar at Antioch University, teaching professional psychology rooted in self-compassion. He is currently leading a project at Google to provide affordable, accessible emotional support to individuals around the world. After a troubled youth, Desmond was exposed to the teachings of Thich Nhat Hanh and eventually studied at Plum Village. Desmond was also a co-organizer of Occupy Wall Street.